N.M.Karamzin's Prose

The Teller in the Tale

A study in narrative technique

By Roger B. Anderson

 CORDOVAN PRESS

HOUSTON

i

The
Teller
in the
Tale

Acknowledgement

I would like to acknowledge my gratitude to Rice University and especially to the Office of the Dean of Humanities for their generous financial assistance in the preparation of the manuscript for this book. For their unstinting help to me during the writing of this work I would like to thank my colleagues Philip Davis, Roy Jones, Robert Patten, Klaus Weissenberger, and James Castañeda.

Contents

For Maureen and the girls, Amy and Jenny

Preface

N. M. Karamzin was born in 1766 to a middle-gentry family in the Simbirsk District of central Russia. His mother died when he was but two and, given the slow pace of rural Russian life in the provinces, literature came to play a most important part in his personality formation. He was especially drawn to the popular moral tales and novels of heroic adventure which were available to him. In their own way, each stimulated his powers of imagination and self-consciousness.

Until the age of eleven Karamzin received no formal education but was tutored at home. In 1777, however, he was enrolled by his father in a private boarding school in Moscow directed by the well known J. M. Schaden, then a professor of philosophy at Moscow University. The youth proved to be a good student, both in acquiring a knowledge of foreign languages (he was particularly good in German), and in the study of moral idealism (both as a philosophical system and in its literary examples). The intellectual level of his studies with Schaden was not significantly different from that expected in courses at the University.

At the age of fifteen, having completed his course of study, Karamzin was placed by his father in the Preobrezhensky Guards, a branch of the army appropriate to his gentry status. A military life was hardly his calling and his years in St. Petersburg, where he was stationed (1781-1784), were more memorable as a time of theatregoing and making friends in the capital's literary salons. Although he did not resign from the army until 1784, most of his time was spent on leave. It is from these years that his fast friendship with the popular sentimental poet I. I. Dmitriev began. It was Dmitriev who first encouraged the younger Karamzin to translate foreign literature seriously.

Karamzin's return to Moscow in 1785 began a period of strong affiliation with the Masons (including such prominent men as N. I. Novikov, I. P. Turgenev [who sponsored him], A. M. Kutuzov, and his close friend A. A. Petrov). His own values centered about a sharpening of pietistic aspirations in himself and the fixed view that man is spiritually perfectable. There already was present in him the notion, both sentimental and Masonic, that only when one is personally pure can he write literature that will exert a positive moral influence on the reader. Although eventually shedding his identification with Russian Masonry, he never lost the movement's sense of the individual's obligation to live by a transcendent creed of moral awareness.

It was typical of Karamzin at this time, however, that his respect for man's personal fulfillment did not translate itself into any social or political program. Like the Masons, his was a quietific philosophy which preached that the individual humbly accept his social lot, whether it be high or low. He shared the Masonic paradox of trying to harmonize a passive accommodation of established social order, complete with serfdom, with a faith in the essential spiritual equality of all men. Compassion and sensitivity were mixed with trust in rigid class stratification as God's intended design for mankind.

In the final analysis Karamzin was more deeply involved with the Masons' practical interests in literature and publishing enterprises than with its religious or mystically philosophical systems. He continued his own apprenticeship as a writer by translating Shakespeare's *Julius Caesar* (1787) and Lessing's *Emilia Golotti* (1788), two of the most popular archetypes for Europe's burgeoning interest in freer dramatic expression. They represented well the attempt to avoid the rigors of neo-classicism's prescriptive staging and limited character psychology. Karamzin's growing interest in making available Europe's new literary taste to the Russian reading public led him into a closer association with Petrov as co-editor of the influential journal *Children's Readings for the Heart and Mind* (from 1787 to 1789). *Children's Readings* contained a mixture of moral didacticism designed for the adolescent and prose appropriate for their parents as well (e.g. Thomson's *The Seasons* and several short stories by Madame de Genlis).

In 1789 Karamzin tested his second-hand knowledge of Western philosophy and literary trends with an extended trip through Europe (Germany, Switzerland, France and England). The fourteen months he spent in travel were to mark both the beginning of his growth as an original writer and his rise to national prominence as the greatest living influence on the reading taste of his countrymen.

During his sojourn he managed to speak with a

number of the most prominent philosophical and literary figures of his time, including Charles Bonnet, J. G. von Herder, J. K. Lavater, J. F. Marmontel, and C. M. Wieland. His success in making the acquaintance of such luminaries made all the more pointed his chagrin at failing to gain an audience with the great Goethe.

Karamzin's direct exposure to the personalities and ideas of his foreign idols, and the very locales they described in their writings, was distilled in his famous *Letters of a Russian Traveler,* which he published serially upon his return. The *Letters* will be treated at length later. Suffice to say here that Karamzin's travels provided a great stimulus for his dedication to propagate at home those precepts of sentimentalism that best harmonized with his faith in enlightenment and technological progress. He was most adept at weaving a wide range of intimately lyrical reveries and nature descriptions among his astute observations on British Parliament, the theoretical weaknesses of French tragedy, or the structure of the Swiss canton. It was a remarkable achievement for the young Karamzin, then but twenty-three.

Upon his return to Russia Karamzin immediately plunged into a flurry of publishing activity. His *Moscow Journal* (1791-1792) was designed as a vehicle for combining translations of significant European sentimental literature and their reviews, along with original Russian works and incidental notes about theatre performances and literary anecdotes. Questions of politics abroad (e.g. the French Revolution) or at home (e.g. the repressive state of Russian censorship) were skirted in favor of less controversial questions of general cultural interest. The *Journal's* openly-expressed intent was to broaden the educated Russian's familiarity with Europe's cosmopolitan way of life while encouraging its emulation at home. Karamzin's editorial policy, which was to avoid publishing theological or mystical writings, both asserted his literary independence and severed his ties with organized Masonry.

It is from this time that such powerful Masonic figures as Kutuzov and Turgenev began their criticism and even vilification of the young author. Even so, the appearance of the enormously popular *Letters* in *Moscow Journal* insured a wide distribution (by Russian standards of the time) to between 250 and 300 paying subscribers. The *Journal's* broad appeal coincided with an obvious need on the part of educated Russia. Its contributors included not only the young devotees of sentimentalism, but the grayer heads of Russian neo-classicism such as the national poets Derzhavin and Kheraskov.

Much of the *Journal's* success had to do with the uniquely expressive language Karamzin developed for his prose. His experimentation with reproducing the conversational ease of polite speech in written Russian opened the way for an approximation of that subtlety in philosophical thought and esthetic refinement of feeling which had bloomed earlier in England, France and Germany. He eliminated old Slavonic forms no longer in common use as well as technical jargon and vulgar speech. At the same time he encouraged the adoption of the sort of calques, loan words and neologisms which blended most easily with Russian sounds. His new style of literary Russian allowed a range of emotional expression unheard of in Russian until his appearance.

The publication of *Moscow Journal* was a clear expression of Karamzin's breadth and balance of optimism. Its vigorous propagation of enlightened culture dovetailed elegantly with a call for the individual to explore his inner emotional and moral potential for experience. Political pressures were simultaneously mounting, however, which were to militate against this popular publishing venture. Catherine the Great's hostility to the Masons occasioned Novikov's imprisonment in 1792. Her fear of the movement's connections with its Western counterparts, especially in Prussia, fitted her general antipathy towards anything that smacked of independent intellectual inquiry. Karamzin, because of his earlier contacts with the Masons and with Novikov in particular, fell under the same cloud of suspicion. Also, it must be remembered, the *Journal's* distribution was much greater by hand than by paid subscription, and Karamzin was not so well off financially that he could personally underwrite its publication when it did not pay for publishing costs.

The year 1793 marked a crisis for the young Karamzin on both personal and political levels. His most intimate friend Petrov died and the rise of the Jacobin Dictatorship in France severely compromised his guarded optimism about the "great experiment" of the French Revolution. Hope, he came to fear, was a fraud; spiritual pain, he was forced to believe, was the real stuff of life. Therefore Karamzin opted for the individual's withdrawal from grand communal pursuits.

With his youthful enthusiasm chilled he left the capital life to which he had contributed so much. Moving to the provinces he became an almost solitary figure. He continued his publishing interests but they were narrower in scope, devoted to imaginative literature exclusively. In 1794 and again in 1795 he produced the literary almanac *Aglaja* in which works of his own composition, both prose and poetry, as well as some quasi-philosophical essays, figured most prominently. His heroes at this stage of his writing career were disenchanted, sensitive men who, in varying degrees, discovered that life lacked moral order and was even hostile to them. He scrupulously avoided all political issues, both by personal inclination and because of the increasing intransigence of Catherine's censorship.

Little is known of Karamzin's personal life during his hermetic country residence in the 1790s. His correspondence with friends (especially with Dmitriev) is characterized by an unspecified Weltschmerz, an elegiac resignation to death coupled with the repeated theme of hope's illusoriness. Some of this melancholia can be attributed to his unsuccessful courtship of the Princess Gagarina. A more substantive reason is his dashed expectation that Paul, who ascended the throne after Catherine's death in 1796, would liberalize the Russian intellectual environment and ease government censorship. It did not take long for the actual extent of Paul's oppressive policies to become known and Russians felt a net of restrictions settle about their rights to free travel abroad and even to receive foreign books. In the light of those odious policies the sense of despair in Karamzin's letters seems all too appropriate. In 1796 and again in 1797 he published issues of his second literary almanac, *Aonidy.* Undoubtedly reflecting the discouraging effects of Paul's anti-intellectualism, Karamzin limited himself to re-publishing pessimistic stories about thwarted personal friendship and love.

Karamzin's inability or unwillingness to write original imaginative prose in the late 1790s led him to try his hand at publishing his *Pantheon of Foreign Literature* in 1798, a compilation of selected classical and modern Western literature. Again the heavy hand of Paul's censors, some of whom personally disliked Karamzin, was revealed. Anything that even hinted at a discussion of republican attitudes or, for that matter, any scrap of inferred anti-monarchist thought, was excluded. A loyal monarchist himself, Karamzin's frustration at such mindless hostility to freedom of thought led him to utter distraction.

It was with a profound sense of relief that Russia witnessed Alexander's coronation as Tsar in 1801, even though it was accomplished at the price of Paul's murder in the very palace. This time a change of monarchs finally carried with it the longed-for atmosphere of political relaxation. Alexander drastically reduced the power of the censors, opened the way for non-gentry classes to legally own land, fostered a proliferation of public schools and universities, and opened the way for Russian intellectuals to communicate freely with their foreign counterparts.

Underlying these and other reforms was a sense that an educated Russian might actually affect the course of Russian society. Karamzin most heartily joined in the rush of enthusiasm. Despite some of his later reservations about the Tsar's diminution of traditional gentry privileges, he remained Alexander's profound admirer until the latter's death in 1825. Karamzin's marriage shortly after Alexander's coronation in 1801 was perhaps indicative of his revived confidence in the future. His founding of his last and greatest journal in 1802, the immensely influential *Messenger of Europe,* is more palpable evidence of that renewed faith. In it Karamzin resurrected and broadened the pursuit of enlightenment and progress which marked his earlier *Moscow Journal.* He mixed translations of Western literature with original contributions, leavening both with selected insightful reviews. He expanded the concept of the *Journal's* cultural section to include for the first time an open forum for the discussion of foreign and domestic politics.

The *Messenger of Europe* continued to exert a formative influence on educated Russia long after Karamzin relinquished his editorship in 1804. It was to be the best and most durable compendium of literary, social and political news and opinion in Russia of the nineteenth century.

From about 1800 there is apparent an increasing interest on Karamzin's part in establishing some sense of Russia's independence, both politically and culturally. His concept of patriotism, which became a staple of his editorial policy in the *Messenger,* subsumes both. It is in that spirit of national pride that he turns to the general question of how a society develops. Choosing a variety of approaches in his last tales, Karamzin explores the profound implications of the individual's relationship with his time and place, be it present or past, in an attempt to assess how they affect one another.

But his interest in social politics, once revived, increasingly led him into the specific question of how Russia emerged from its turbulent historical mix into a recognizable society, into its nationhood. His search for those formative links with the past came at an appropriate time. Even though Russia was beginning to play a major role in Western political and military affairs it still had no coherent chronicle of its own past. Karamzin's inclination towards historical pursuits is apparent in his last tale "Martha the Mayoress" (1803). There he sought to reproduce the sense of a crucial moment of conflict in his country's past whose resolution helped form national destiny. The sense of registering significant past events, together with their psychological impact on national figures who experienced them, brought together Karamzin's talents as an imaginative writer, historical researcher and social philosopher. He was to exercise those talents in concert for the rest of his life while he wrote his *History of the Russian State.*

In 1803 he petitioned Alexander for official

approval of the project and received the Tsar's commission that same year. He abandoned *belles lettres* to devote himself solely to historical investigations. It was a tremendous undertaking, and Karamzin became more and more a dweller in the archives of Moscow and St. Petersburg. He thought that his History would take only a few years to complete. It was a most unrealistic estimate. As it happened, he finished eleven volumes and got no further than the Time of Troubles which attended the end of the Rurik dynasty in the late sixteenth century. He died while working on the twelfth volume.

As Karamzin worked on his *History* his relations with Alexander were often strained to the point of breaking. The author persisted in opposing the liberal trappings of the monarch's (and his favorite Speransky's) reforms. As Karamzin read more about his country's autocratic past and compared it to the recent republican upheavals in France, he became increasingly convinced of the need for the kind of domestic order he saw available only in the reign of a strong Tsar. Predictably, he was also an admirer of Napoleon's restoration of autocratic rule in France a few years earlier. Thus Karamzin found himself in the paradoxical position of being devoted to Alexander's right to rule by edict while at the same time openly criticizing those edicts when they portended a liberalized distribution of authority.

Alexander's reaction to his official historian was also mixed. His displeasure was often pointed and open. For example, he forced Karamzin to wait more than a month for an audience when the first eight volumes of the *History* were ready for official presentation in 1816. Despite his reactionary politics Karamzin simultaneously inspired the Tsar's grudging respect for the unquestioned honesty of conviction with which the *History* was written. Indeed, it would have been embarrassing to Alexander to disown the history he himself had commissioned, especially when it proved to be extremely popular with the public (the first printing of 3,000 copies for those eight volumes was completely sold out in less than a month when it finally appeared in 1818). A kind of balance, touched with affection, was gradually achieved between autocrat and author which endured until Alexander's death in 1825, followed by Karamzin's own demise within a few months.

Introduction

As literary critic, esthetician, poet, political philosopher, historian and reformer of the literary language, Karamzin left an encyclopedic legacy in his country which exerted a strong influence well past his death.[1] The multiple aspects of this influence become increasingly impressive as more study of the late eighteenth and early nineteenth centuries accumulates.[2] It is as a writer of non-historical prose, however, that Karamzin is best known. His adaptation of popular sentimental themes and his distinctive plaiting of melancholy moods with descriptions of physical settings have become synonomous with his name. "Poor Liza" is the best example of that side of Karamzin's talent and the tale's appearance in numerous anthologies, both Russian and Western, has traditionally determined the general reader's acquaintance with him.

However, the Russian's range and development of non-historical prose goes well beyond the ubiquitous "Poor Liza" and its lugubrious trappings. He experimented with theme and character as long as he wrote. He created the first serious Russian historical tale ("Martha the Mayoress") along with Gothic suspense tales (e.g., "Bornholm Island"). He can be credited with producing a prototype of the Russian *Bildungsroman* (i.e., "Knight of our Time"). His sustained reliance there on objective observation and his experimentation with developing biographical and psychological motivation in the hero were highly innovative for Russia at the dawn of the nineteenth century. Karamzin's choice of theme runs the gamut from Masonic faith in ideal happiness beyond the grave to Sternian playfulness; from Ossianic despair to detached curiosity about the developing mind of a boy; from moral tales of family happiness to the serious portrayal of a formative stage in Russia's evolution as a viable society.

This book treats Karamzin's major prose fiction which was written between the years 1791 and 1803: *Letters of a Russian Traveler* (published irregularly between 1791-1801), and the more important tales including "Poor Liza" ("Bednaja Liza") [1792], "Natalia the Boyar's Daughter" ("Natal'ja bojarskaja dočʹ") [1792], "The Beautiful Princess and the Fortunate Dwarf" ("Prekrasnaja carevna i ščastlivyj karla") [1792], "Julia" ("Julija") [1794], "Bornholm Island" ("Ostrov Borngolʹm") [1794], "Sierra Morena" ("Sierra-Morena") [1795], "My Confession" ("Moja ispovedʹ") [1802], "Knight of Our Time" ("Rycarʹ našego vremeni") [1802], "The Sensitive and the Cold" ("Čuvstvitelʹnyj i xolodnyj") [1803], and "Martha the Mayoress" ("Marfa posadnica") [1803]. Karamzin's prose works which were written before his travels abroad (1789-1790) are certainly worthy of scrutiny but they lie outside the scope of this study. There is a systematic, even rhythmical growth in his mature literary method which stands out most clearly in

the time frame provided by his *Letters* as a starting point
and "Martha the Mayoress" as an end. Not treated here in
any primary sense are specific questions concerning
Karamzin's extensive reliance on several contemporary
Western sources for many of his themes and models for
character drawing. Two recent books[3] on the Russian have
successfully discussed his thorough familiarity with the
foremost thinkers, writers and esthetic movements of the
eighteenth century in Western Europe.

My purpose here is to discuss Karamzin's non-
historical prose chronologically and systematically on
the level of an intrinsic (textual) analysis. Emphasis is
placed, first, on dividing that body of prose into coherent
stages, each of which reflects unique ideational concerns.
Second, I have attempted to point out the particulars of
narrative method characteristic of each cycle or stage for
Karamzin's choice of narrative angle is intimately tied to
the kinds of issues he raises. Karamzin evolved rapidly as a
thinker and artist, and each stage of his evolution exhibits
a pronounced coherence which results from his coordination of subject matter and narrative point of view. Within
any group of tales there is more consistency in Karamzin's
narrative perspective than in his selection of genre.
"Natalia the Boyar's Daughter," for example, is a light
pseudo-historical tale with an emphasis on verbal wit.
"Julia," considered here as part of the same cycle, is a
serious moral tale set in contemporary society. "A Knight
of Our Time" presents significant personal influences in
the formation of a child's psyche. As such its genre is quite
distinct from "The Sensitive and the Cold" which follows
the late eighteenth century's fascination with contrasting
unalterably opposed and static personality types. Yet both
these tales share internal similarities which are best ascer-
tained by a discussion of Karamzin's choice of the same

narrative angles in each. The task of assessing the coherence of each stage, as well as the progression of those stages, is necessary to understand adequately and appreciate Karamzin's versatility and growth as a prose writer.

The basic thesis of this study, then, is simply that Karamzin's choice of narrative point(s) of view in any given piece of fiction relates significantly to the unified message of that work. The source of narration necessarily interacts with the work's overall structure, including its system of values, its character production, and its physical descriptions of people and places. Everything the reader receives from a piece of fiction is necessarily shaped by the narrative perspective(s) indigenous to that work. Point of view serves the work's implied values and affects them directly by its specific mode of expression. Each narrative point of view functions as a center for organizing what Lionel Trilling calls "the background buzz of implication" which goes into a work of fiction.[4]

Wayne Booth perceives the selection and arrangement of those narrative centers as contributing necessarily to some overall rhetorical design in a given piece of fiction.[5] Each narrative perspective has its peculiar properties and limitations, and the perspective's function flows from those properties and limitations. A narrator, with his distinctions of finite personality, cannot claim the undisputed authority of an author who interrupts the narrative to comment on his own literary production, explaining what it *really* means. A commenting author cannot involve the reader emotionally in a described experience as successfully as can a narrator who purports to have either witnessed that experience or lived through it himself. Neither of these narrative sources has traditionally aspired to that illusion of objectively accumulated fact and physical detail ("showing" vs. "telling") as has third person narration. The structure of discernable points of view in a work, then, is intimately related to how the reader perceives the events and characters which populate the fabula of that work. As Lubomir Doležel, the contemporary Czech theorist on point of view, aphoristically says: "The speaker [any one of a number of narrative voices] is an intrinsic organizing and integrating factor of the text structure." [6]

Throughout my assessment of Karamzin's prose I have sought to keep sight of the central question of point of view and its fundamental relation to the system of values inherent in each piece of Karamzin's fiction I treat. This approach has the distinct advantage of providing consistent formal criteria for following the pronounced evolution of ideational concerns characteristic of Karamzin's prose. There are, for example, extensive changes in the basic theme of unfulfilled love when "Poor Liza" and "Sierra Morena" are compared. The different ways Karamzin handles questions of character development in relation to a historical context in "Natalia" is quite different from his representation of them in "Martha." Analyzing each tale in terms of its own narrative scheme provides a sensitive index to Karamzin's change as a writer. By implication it can also trace his changing attitudes toward life.

The object of this book is not theoretical but practical. Norman Friedman, one of the foremost American students of narrative technique, has already worked out adequate terminology for distinguishing different narrative points of view. [7] That terminology is widely accepted and I use it in this book, not only as a matter of convenience, but because the tools fit the task. Friedman's discussion of narrative modes traces a continuum in authority within the narrative process. The most authoritative is "editorial omniscience;" the least authoritative is the illusion of "slice of life" or the "camera mode," (i.e., without apparent interpretation or selection of information in any way). In Karamzin's case there are basically three distinct points of view which function as organizing sources within the narrative flow. These include "editorial omniscience," "neutral omniscience," and the narrator (in Friedman's terminology, either "narrator-as-witness," or "narrator-as-protagonist"). The more sophisticated models of "untrustworthy" narrators, the ironic handling of narrative angles, or the playing off of contradictory points of view are more appropriate to a period in Russian literature much more recent than that of the late eighteenth century.

In editorial omniscience, the Olympian voice of the author-construct involves itself directly with the reader, conversing with him in asides and digressions. This "intruding author" stands in the wings of the work, periodically revealing himself as its creator to tell the reader what is right and wrong, true and false. He exercises direct control over the reader's formation of opinions through auctorial directives and points him toward the desired interpretation of what happens in the work. This narrative mode is traditionally bound to expounding moral principles on a general scale and its marked presence in the eighteenth century was meant to have an edifying influence on the European reader. I. Z. Sherwood, in her study of the British novel of the period, explains the author's intrusive habit as a continuation of the didactic impulse behind the moral essay, one of the favorite genres of the eighteenth century in England.[8] She provides an example of the commenting author in the following quote from Fielding's *Tom Jones:*

> Indeed the sensations of pleasure it [i.e., a sanguine temperament] gives are much more

> constant, as well as much keener, than those which that blind lady [Fortune] bestows; Nature having wisely contrived that some satiety and languor should be annexed to all our real enjoyments, lest we should be so taken up by them as to be stopped from further pursuits. [9]

As in the passage above, editorial omniscience tends to be more formal in tone than the surrounding narration [10] because of its overriding didactic intentions and the author's desire to elevate those remarks to a more dignified status, to draw attention to them.

A step away from editorial omniscience is what Friedman terms "neutral omniscience." In this case, the self-conscious author's voice and personal directives are absent, but the reader is nevertheless told facts which he has no cause to doubt. The author renders information, facts, descriptions and interpretations the reader readily accepts as true, but they do not come from the identifiable personality of the author. They "speak for themselves."

There are inherently two variations of neutral omniscient narration. On the one hand there is the sort of objective information which is necessary, both for clarity in cause-and-effect relationships, and for the arrangement of scenic props. The sentence: "Liza went into Moscow every day to sell flowers" presents a kind of communication which is itself non-interpretive. The mode fills in gaps between scenes; it provides necessary background or summary data and facilitates a clear ordering of facts which might be useful later in the work. On the other hand, neutral omniscience often carries unquestioned interpretations, but without the author's revealed presence. With some alterations the above sentence reads: "Liza was a *dutiful* daughter and went into Moscow every day in the *fervent* hope of earning enough money to support her mother, *whom Liza loved with her whole heart."* This information is, of course, slanted, as indicated by the italicized qualifying remarks. Yet it still presents situations and characters in terms of uncontroverted facts which also proceed from an omniscient source. The two potentials of this mode are not always clearly distinguishable and both may appear in the same paragraph or even the same sentence. Its essential distinction from other narrative points of view, however, remains its presentation of information as given facts within the context of the work and the lack of an identifiable personality (author or character) taking direct responsibility for it.

Proceeding yet further away from the construct of the identifiable author, there is the narrator: the "I-as-witness" and the related "I-as-protagonist." In each, a center of consciousness contains the recognizable idiosyncracies and limitations of a structured personality, be he observer or participant in the story. The peculiarities of his tastes, habits, etc. enter into his narrative duties and color his presentation of other characters (as well as of himself), events and settings. Here, instead of the superior author who possesses oracular powers, a mortal character within the work takes on the narrative task. The important distinction separating him from the other two modes is his fallibility. The intruding author has full knowledge about everyone and everything he describes; neutral omniscience bears the same stamp of *ex cathedra.* The narrator, however, carries within himself "no more than ordinary access to the mental states of other." [11] He is therefore prone to blur the events he describes by adding his own subjective associations and psychological quirks. The most quoted example of a Karamzinian narrator and his visible personality is in "Poor Liza" when he says: "Ach! I love those subjects which touch my heart and make me cry tears of tender grief!''

The narrator entails the often-mentioned quality of implied sincerity. One of the mode's main attributes is its appeal to the reader's sympathy and personal sense of identification. Bertil Romberg, in his book on the question of first person narration in the novel, emphasizes this asset of credibility surrounding the narrator. [12] Being such a personalized source of narration, the narrator usually succeeds in binding the reader to his own emotional slant on what he describes. [13] The appearance of the narrator as a distinct and limited consciousness, freed from the intruding author's penchant to preach general truths, is historically one of the salient features of growing sentimental and romantic taste in the late eighteenth century.

Varying combinations of these narrative points of view typify Karamzin's prose works. When there are multiple sources of narration in a given work, Karamzin tends to organize them so as to accentuate one while the others assume subordinate and supportive roles relative to the central mode. Some of his tales, on the other hand, are presented almost exclusively from one narrative source. In all cases, however, Karamzin's use of each narrative mode reflects the traditional characteristics associated with it as described above.

The division of Karamzin's prose works presented here basically follows the chronology of their appearance in print. A separate chapter is devoted to the *Letters* because of its complex system of genres and its length. There are two continuous strands of meaning in the *Letters.* Each develops according to its own thematic potential and each is characterized by different narrative schemes. These two parts are examined in terms of their separate contributions to Karamzin's broadly educative design, for it is that design which comprises the great unity of the work.

The tales tend to fall into three groups, each with its own ideational emphases and its own narrative schemes. The first group is composed of "Poor Liza," "Natalia the Boyar's Daughter," "The Beautiful Princess and the Fortunate Dwarf," and "Julia." Editorial omniscience functions in each to organize and interpret the events of the particular tale. Other points of view are subordinated to it. The second group includes "Bornholm Island," "Sierra Morena," and "My Confession." Here the main narrative source is that of the narrator (the narrator-observer in "Bornholm Island" and the narrator-protagonist in the latter two). The last cycle contains "A Knight of Our Time," "The Sensitive and the Cold," and "Martha the Mayoress." In these Karamzin conducts different experiments with the structural potential of the neutral omniscient mode in relation to the more traditional intruding author. "A Knight" and "The Sensitive and the Cold" have much in common in their coordination of these narrative perspectives and are considered here as a naturally contrastive unit. In "Martha the Mayoress" Karamzin develops both neutral omniscience and editorial omniscience in accordance with heroic or epic forms to accommodate his development of the historical tale.

1

Art as Education

Karamzin's publication of *Pis'ma russkogo putešest-vennika [Letters of a Russian Traveler]* which appeared serially during 1791-1801 was a literary and cultural event of the first magnitude in Russia. [1] For the first time [2] a Russian prepared a thorough and engaging depiction of life in the Western countries which appealed to his educated countrymen. The chief reason for Karamzin's success was his adroit intertwining of reliable facts about the West, simultaneously balanced with refined feelings and judgments about what he saw. The combination carried all before it and the *Letters* long served as the model for numerous imitations by other Russian writers. [3]

A brief look at the stage of Russia's cultural development at the close of the eighteenth century shows how Karamzin's travel notes fitted the needs and demands of his readers. Everywhere one is reminded of Russia's infatuation with Western cultural taste. Catherine II's short-lived period of liberalization, her correspondence with French philosophers of the Enlightenment, her passing flirtation with the possibility of implementing the *Nakaz* which owed much to Western liberalism, the copying of Western bureaucratic forms, the gentry's dependence on the French language, all testify to Russia's fascination with the more sophisticated and enlightened accomplishments of the West. Yet, most educated Russians had seen very little of the life they took as their model. Very few had first hand knowledge of its universities, its art treasures, or even its geography. In a broad cultural sense Karamzin's *Letters* proved a veritable cornucopia of facts about several areas of Western life.

In literature, Russia's imitation of foreign forms was as pronounced as in other cultural areas. The wave of sentimentalism, which had been gradually swelling in the West since the 1730s, broke over Russia at its peak, while neo-classicism was still viable as a standard of literary taste. The new questions of man's exploration of his extra-rational faculties, self analysis, visions of strong emotion, melancholy contemplation of one's finitude, the measurement of a man's worth by how easily he could shed tears — all ideas and *topoi* of the new literary taste — bombarded the Russian reader at once.

Sentimentalism as a philosophy and literary movement came late to Russia and, like earlier esthetic forms in the eighteenth century, was largely derivative of Western theorists and practitioners. The *Letters* effectively integrated and forcefully displayed many of the important tenets of sentimentalism (as discussed below) both in their theory and in the form of numerous examples. The movement generally was a reaction to the formal logic and character typology of neo-classical thought and denied the supposition that man is perfectible through the efficient ordering of his society. Substituting man the individual for

neo-classicism's concept of man the social integer, sentimentalism opened the whole question of the human
personality, how the individual views himself, his society
and nature. The eternal questions of meaning in life,
morality and beauty were considerations that sensibility
opened to personal inquiry. Rationalism's *a priori* definitions and value judgments concerning basic philosophical
issues were called into question as sentimentalism gathered
force in Europe of the eighteenth century.

As a reflection of the late eighteenth-century's loss
of faith in neo-classicism's assumptions about logic, society
and man's homogenous character, sentimentalism carried
with it a sense of estrangement in the individual from his
society as a codified system. There was a general decline in
the belief that major problems of life could be seen, let
alone solved, by traditional political or educational institutions. The sentimentalist therefore sought alternatives to
the materialistic ordering of life. Under the influence of
imagination he often resorted to an imagined Golden Age
of some past, morally superior time when man was pure,
untrammeled by politics, living in perpetual accord with
his brothers. Sometimes he sought respite in an equally
mythologized vision of primitive peoples who were graced
with an innate wisdom and nobility, far superior to that of
his own sophisticated society with all its technological
proficiency and intellectual pride.

Most often the sentimentalist resorted to the more
available refuge of uncultivated nature. He sought to com-
mune with it and drink in its non-verbal wisdom by giving
himself over to its slower rhythm of life. He saw nature as
eternal while man's architectural and commercial produc-
tions he considered transitory and inferior. Nature
answered the sensitive man's desire to escape the ostenta-
tious and petty pursuits of the city. It was a balm to his

inner sense of futility and pessimism; it offered "natural" pleasures and beauty as alternatives to the bankrupt promises of contemporary society.

Central to sentimental considerations is the whole issue of reality and how it is perceived. Rather than the single-storeyed vision of neo-classicism in which reality is a materialist conception, objectively the same for all who view it, the sentimentalist took a subjective approach. Reality for him was a function of his unique personality and its interplay with external things and people. His private mood, the product of that interplay at a given time, was his measure of reality. As a result, spontaneity of feeling in a single individual became a standard for sentimentalism. There was no room for the philosophe's formal logic; it gave way to a new-found fascination with associational psychology and the labyrinth of the individual's inner thoughts and feelings. The cult of feeling required no rational explanation; it was self-justifying. It was the new man's vehicle for exploring the possibilities of his private imagination, the subtleties of a whole range of exciting emotions. Feeling was all in sensibility. Its devotee relied on it for distinguishing right from wrong since, for him, it was the only sure path to truth and morality. One's capacity to be touched by the beauty of nature or one's ability to enter emotionally into the problems and joys of a friend were sure indices of one's worth. Sensitivity to poignant emotion led to wisdom for the sentimentalist as abstract logic had sought to do for the neo-classicist.

Esthetics in art was also dominated by the cult of feeling. The artist's chief requisite was that he must have an open and feeling heart. Without it he had no right to compose. Since sensibility was the only sure way to wisdom and virtue, the author himself must possess its blessings in order to depict them adequately in his characters.[4] There were no announced rules for writing "good" literature other than the presence of the author's capacity to fuse his own personality with the descriptive or narrative task. Art was less a craft than the natural product of private inspiration. The author often joined in the spirit of freely expressed emotion by assuming the ego form of a narrator. He verged on becoming a character himself, a revolutionary concept given the mandatory distance between creator and his work in neo-classical poetics.

The pervasive emphasis on feeling in the new literature fostered a democratic tendency, both in character choice and in the author's relationship with the reader. Characters tended to come from lower economic groups (the emerging middle class and sometimes the peasantry). Since everyone had the innate capacity to feel, the way was clear to choose simple people as heroes and heroines, or mix the classes in the thematics of love. The old categories in neo-classical esthetics that relegated different social groups to different literary genres disintegrated in sentimental literature. All people, supposedly, were potentially open to the same emotions. Nobility became a relative quality, more a function of a character's personal sensitivity than of any class consideration. Sentimentalism made a standard of lovers, united by a common feeling, but thwarted by outmoded class segregation or rigid social tradition.

The new disenchantment with logic as a panacea resulted in a good deal of pessimism, often taking the form of personal alienation from traditional social goals and modes of thought. The new man retreated into a world of his own making, sometimes alone, sometimes with a coterie of friends who shared his disillusionment. He relished his private contemplation of life's futility and communed with the ruins of the past, seeing in them a reminder of the decay that surely awaited his own society. His mood was typified by a melancholic belief that life beguiled man with hope only to destroy that hope before it could bear fruit. Life was unreliable at best and wisdom lay in attuning one's heart to recognize frustrated desire as a necessary fact of existence. The sentimentalist looked instead to an alternate order, a morality that could over-arch the disappointments of this life. The sensitive individual might be doomed to tears in his earthly existence but he could still hope for a better life beyond the grave in which injustice and betrayed dreams would be reconciled. That expectation lent a sweetness to his melancholy and often bred passivity toward social and economic problems of the here-and-now, thereby furthering the sentimenta-list's withdrawal from ordinary social and material pur-suits. It helped him make sense of the disenchantment and alienation that he felt growing within him.

Sentimentalism, then, helped the growth of alterna-tives to traditional social categories. The cult of feeling was founded on a new vision of human worth and relied on the guiding wisdom of feeling and personalized morals. Faith in life, when it existed at all, sprang from the ineffable genius of the heart. Living came to be a broadly inductive process for the individual in the sentimental scheme of things. One found truth through introversion and esta-blished a sense of reality through the promptings of imagi-nation. The new man came to seek his own way in life beyond the pale of social categories. [5]

The sentimental considerations sketched above were the product of decades of maturation in the West. England contributed its Sterne, Richardson, Thomson, Gray and Macpherson. France made its offering through Rousseau, Marivaux and Prevost. Germany had its Goethe, Kant (in his late moralist writings), Gessner, Herder and Lavater.

The full impact of their combined thought and work made itself known in Russia almost as a monolithic force. Its influence was irresistible.

Translations of popular sentimental novelists like Richardson and Prevost became available for Russian readers in limited quantities from around 1760.[6] As crude as they were (Richardson's novels usually found their way into Russia by way of uninspired French translations) they touched off a flurry of ambitious but pale imitations.[7] V. V. Sipovsky, a most thorough critic of Russian prose in the eighteenth century, summarizes such works, along with their numerous contemporaries, as frankly plagiaristic of the sentimental novel in narrative method (usually based on an exchange of letters), setting and themes.[8] The Russian intelligentsia was literally carried away by an esthetic standard it could barely imitate.[9] Just as even the fairly well-educated Russian was largely uninformed about the museums, legislatures and mountain ranges of Western Europe, so was he but vaguely aware of what constituted the esthetics and philosophy that formed the sentimental movement.

It was Karamzin's *Letters* which bridged the lamentable gap in Russia's general knowledge of Western culture and, especially, of sentimentalism. By the publication of his notes he presented a breadth of information about the varied facts and customs of foreign life unseen before in his homeland. His sensitive perception of the West's sophisticated philosophical and literary interest in sentimentalism similarly enabled him to capture the spirit of the West's explosion of experimentation and change. The *Letters* is thus a hybrid form of the travel notes and represents two distinct lines of interest on Karamzin's part.

In one respect the work represents a highly authentic cultural and physical description of life and manners in the major countries of the West. This level of the work contains well-organized representations of European architecture, art treasures, legislative practices, theatres, national monuments and nature's more interesting scenes. Karamzin also went into the specifics of eating habits, street scenes, and what kinds of hospitality typified each country he visited. Such a painstaking profile of Europe provided an immense service to the Russian reading public and greatly widened the window onto the West which Peter the Great first forcibly opened almost a century earlier. Sipovsky, in his exhaustive study of the *Letters,* sees the greatest value of the work in its stimulating effect on Russia's burgeoning interest in the cultural data of the West. [10] These sections of the *Letters,* treating a cross-section of Western life, are highly objectified and contain only as much of the traveler's personality as is necessary to give a semblance of verisimilitude. Here Karamzin systematically removes the impression of a feeling or judgmental presence within the description process. Cultural data, statistics, dimensions, precise details within pictorial scenes are primary here. In such passages Karamzin is more the intellectually curious man than the introverted and lyrical sentimentalist.

On the second level, the *Letters* carries the stamp of a sensitive commentator who is prone to dwell on his reactions to the places and events he describes. In these passages Karamzin's detached curiosity and impersonal descriptive practices give way to an intricate system of digressions from the basic description process. External reality functions here as a catalyst for the expression of personal feelings and opinions. [11] On this level Karamzin arranges his impressions into subjective structures which are distinguished by his tone of vigorous involvement with what he sees and does.

The montage effect of the *Letters*, partaking of both tendencies mentioned above, is striking. Critics have long viewed the work as virtually two different documents, intertwined, but each with its own purpose and function. Soviet critics are prone to commend one document (the cultural profile) as "realistic" and look askance at the other (Karamzin's exploration of his own subjectivity) as self-indulgent in its introspection and, therefore, "unrealistic." [12] Each document can sustain critical interest in its hermetic isolation, but the work as a whole suffers from such dismemberment. There is a unity of effect in the *Letters* based on an overall didactic design. The *Letters* as a whole responds to the overwhelming need of the Russian reader to learn about the West. Each of the two "documents" traditionally discerned in his work presents a thorough assessment of different facets of European civilization. Karamzin presents an external transcription of objective facts about Western life (whether it be a listing of museums in Dresden, legislative practices in London or waterfalls around Geneva). He also develops his own understanding of the philosophical and esthetic ideals of sentimentalism which had been emerging from beneath the surface of that culture, inspiring its art and exciting imitation in his own Russia. Each part of his notes has its own rhythm of exposition and explanation, its own vocabulary and its own appeals. Each document reflects different features of the same flow of information and of values then moving from the West into Russia.

Because Karamzin teaches various kinds of lessons he chooses different narrative perspectives to accommodate each. On one hand, as has been pointed out, he presents a wealth of specific data about life in the West. Since the writer's problem here is one of accuracy in transcription, Karamzin chooses what we now call neutral omniscience as his prime narrative modus. It is effective in establishing clear cause-and-effect relationships and in conveying objective information. Neutral omniscience precisely suits Karamzin's descriptive purpose in those sections of the notes.

On the other hand, Karamzin also teaches his Russian readers to appreciate the major suppositions of Western sentimentalism (i.e., how man relates his environment, the outer world, to his inner realm of private experiences). For Karamzin this is a question of forming opinion, not of description for its own sake. To produce a rounded and forceful introduction to those sentimental attitudes and beliefs, Karamzin relies on a combination of narrative points of view — editorial omniscience and the personalized narrator (a mixture of "I-as-observer" and "I-as-protagonist"). Each narrative mode here contributes to the didactic effect. When Karamzin seeks to make clear some sentimental principle, he relies on editorial omniscience, appealing to the reader's conceptual faculties. When Karamzin adopts the guise of a personal, experiencing narrator, he encourages his reader to share his subjective interpretation of an event, character or object. The appeal is to the reader's feelings, his ability to enter emotionally into the narrator's own inner lyrical state. It is no coincidence that Karamzin's lyrical interpretations consistently restate the opinions and judgment he delivers in editorial omniscience at various points in the *Letters.* Plying his readers with the time-honored rhetorical program of repeating significant opinions in various forms (intellectual and emotional), Karamzin develops a tightly organized and highly effective apology for the new sensibility.

The two sides of the *Letters,* while ultimately complementary in their didactic intent, are most clearly seen when they are separated. That separation does some violence to the elegantly smooth mingling Karamzin creates between the parts. It is necessary to make the cleavage, however, in order to discern more clearly the method by which Karamzin realizes the different potentials of the work.

First, there are those sections, presented in neutral omniscience, which are devoted to objective descriptions of Western life. A. Galakhov, a noted Russian critic of the *Letters* late in the nineteenth century, emphasizes the accumulation of factually detailed accounts of Western life in the notes. Things, places and events are presented in dispassionate and ordered clarity; nothing halts the flow of uncontroverted facts. One has the sensation of reading a transcript of what is to be seen in Europe by anyone who visits the places Karamzin describes.

The extent of the objectification effect stands out clearly in the catalog of devices by which Karamzin screens the reader from the personality of his narrator. For example, the literary historian N. S. Tikhonravov has pointed out that Karamzin took entire sections from existing travel guides and other tourist literature, representing them as original observations. [13] In using standardized pictorial descriptions, Karamzin de-emphasizes any sense of spontaneity or originality within the narration. His use of foreign language citations contributes to the same illusion of objectivity. In more than fifty places he makes reference to a place, object or local custom both in Russian and in the language of the country he is visiting. A language doublet results which renders the object more concrete to the reader. There is usually no subjective value in the doublet; it acts rather as a means of guaranteeing the reader a precise understanding of some interesting fact for its own sake. For example, he gives a German place name in Russian, *zelenaja kladovaja,* adding the German original in parentheses *das Grüne Gewölbe.* In the description of Baden Karamzin gives the Roman place name *Aquae Helveticae,* promptly adding the Russian translation, *Gel'-vetskie vody.* In England he provides an example of British local color by citing, in the original, the public notice: *Take care of your pockets!* Again, he follows the foreign expression with a Russian translation, *Beregite karmany!* In each of these examples as in his general use of the device (there are over thirty) Karamzin clarifies some cultural fact of Western Europe for his Russian audience, much as an efficient and impersonal guide might do.

A more complex method of eliminating the narrator's personality from many descriptions results from Karamzin's regular shift of the narrative voice from the first person to a more generalized form. For example:

Iz sada prošli my v park, gde vstrečaetsja glazam japonskij domik na levoj storone glavnoj allei; a dalee, perešedši čerez kamennyj most, vidiš' na obeix storonax prekrasnye xramiki. [14]

[From the garden we went into a park where there greets the eye a small Japanese house on the left side of the main path; then further, after crossing a stone bridge, you see beautiful little temples on both sides.]

Beginning with a reference to himself as narrator (the first person plural *my*) Karamzin quickly switches into the third person impersonal form *(vstrečaetsja glazam)* and then into the second person singular which, in this context, is also impersonal (the use of the verb *vidiš'* without a pronoun corresponds here to the English "one"). [15]

In another example, the narrator initiates the description in his own voice: *Ne budu opisyvat'vam naružnosti sego kvadratnogo zamka, . . .* ["I won't describe the exterior of this square castle to you, . . ."] (p. 411), then shifts into the generalized second person singular and completes the description: *Xočeš'imet' kartiny, éstamp lučšix masterov, v ramax, za steklami, podi tuda i vybiraj."* [If you want pictures, prints of the finest masters, in frames behind glass, go there and choose,"] (p. 411). The impersonal quality of this quote is particularly conspicuous because the mythical correspondents to whom he is writing are addressed as *vy* ["you"] in the preceding paragraph while the second person singular form (without the pronoun) appears in this passage, again carrying the meaning of "one" or "anyone."

Instances of the voice shift are numerous and they often occur within a single sentence. In some cases the first person changes into the third person impersonal form. In one example the narrator, as usual, begins with some personal remark which identifies him as the describer (e.g., what he has just eaten, with whom he dined, how much he has enjoyed himself, etc.). There is then an abrupt switch into a totally impersonal description of an art museum in Dresden, handled completely in the third person (neutral omniscient mode). The account is filled with minute and often technical facts about twenty paintings, together with the biographies and basic techniques of the thirteen artists represented. Sounding like a lecturer in an abbreviated art course, complete with extensive footnotes, Karamzin effectively eliminates all lyrical potential from the long passage (pp. 145-149).

In other cases Karamzin mixes all three voices (first,

second and third person). Beginning the description of Boulogne with the usual intimate *ja* ["I"], Karamzin remarks: *Skol'ko raz byl ja v Bulonskom lesu, ne vidav slavnoj "Bezdelki"! Segodni videv ee, xvalil vkus xozjaina, žalel o nynešnej sud'be ego.* ["How many times have I been in the Boulogne forest without seeing the remarkable Bagatelle! Having seen it today, I praised the owner's taste and regretted its fate at present."] (p. 482). After four lines in the narrator's own voice, Karamzin casts off his guise of witnessing personality and gets down to the objective, almost pedantic job of cataloging the art objects present. Third person narration, laced with passive constructions, dominates the next twenty-two lines: *U kryl'ca stoit mramornaja nimfa i deržit na golove korzinu s cvetami; v étu korzinu stavitsja noč'ju xrustal'nyj fonar' dlja osveščenija kryl'ca...* ["At the entrance stands a marble nymph holding on its head a basket of flowers; a crystal lamp is placed in this basket for the entrance's illumination..."] (pp. 482-483). With two short inclusions of narration in the second person plural: *Nakonec vy uznaete, čto étot pavil'jon est' v samon dele volšebnyj, ...* ["Finally you will learn that this pavilion really is enchanted, ..."], and: *vidite malen'kij domik* ["you see a small house"], Karamzin returns to the third person for the remaining paragraphs. Thus, after beginning the scene in the voice of the narrator, Karamzin conducts about ninety per cent of the scene in neutral omniscience.

The various shifting patterns of narrative perspective in these and other descriptions point to a single effect. While the narrator may be nominally present, Karamzin has a distinct tendency to move into the more generalized narrative forms, shedding his personal presence in the process. His weakening of the narrator as a personality focuses attention on objects and cultural facts for their own sake. Meyer Abrams' analogy of the mirror and the lamp points up the principle clearly. Karamzin "mirrors" the physical world and its specific facts by excluding most personal interpretations and subjective meaning the objects might hold for the describer. [16]

Karamzin employs a writing style on this level of the travel notes which is distinguished by its economy of statement and emphasis on objective detail. Here is an example of an account of life in Zurich. It is representative of more than sixty other passages dealing with the four countries Karamzin describes:

> V Cirixskom kantone ščitaetsja okolo 180 000 žitelej, a v gorode — okolo 10 000, no tol'ko dve tysjači imejut pravo graždanstva, izbirajut sudej, učastvujut v pravlenii i proizvod- jat torg; vse pročie lišeny sej vygody. Iz tridcati cexov, na kotorye razdeleny graždane, odin nazyvaetsja glavnym, ili dvorjanskim, imeja pered drugimi to preimuščestvo, čto iz nego vybiraetsja v členy verxovnogo soveta os'mnad- cat' čelovek, — iz pročix že tol'ko po dvenadcati. (p. 243)

> [In the Zurich canton there are about 180,000 inhabitants while in the city there are about 10,000; but only two thousand have the right of citizenship, select judges, participate in its government and conduct trade; all others are deprived of this advantage. Out of the thirty guilds, among which the citizens are distributed, one is called the chief or noble guild, and has the advantage over the others that eighteen from it are selected to be members of the upper council.

From the others there are selected only twelve each.]

The passage relies heavily on substantives. The only adjectives included are those needed to convey technical specificity. There are almost no epithets capable of projecting a personal reaction to what is described, neither does Karamzin judge what he transcribes. He concentrates on conveying exact detail in as economical a style as possible. The central importance of the noun and its burden of compressed fact in the passage creates a string of tangible relationships whose existence and function are independent of the describer. The role Karamzin establishes for himself here is, as Blagoy says, a quiet tone of emotional equanimity and personal neutrality. [17]

E. G. Kovalevskaya, a modern Soviet commentator on Karamzin's prose style, indicates that most of his borrowed vocabulary and calques come from semi-technical sources and are laden with specific, denotative meaning. [18] These objective descriptions also incorporate a high incidence of participles whose widespread use is virtually synonymous with bookish writing. Significantly, their presence is negligible in the narrator's lyrical descriptions. My italicizing of participles in a typical passage of objective description accentuates their concentration:

V zdešnej ratuše, *nazyvaemoj* Rimljaninom (*Römer*), pokazyvajut putešestvennikam tu zalu v kotoroj obedaet *novoizbrannyj* imperator i gde stojat portrety vsex imperatorov, ot Konrada I do Karla VI. Kto ne požaleet červonca, tot tam že v arxive možet videt i slavnuju 'Zolotuju bullu,' ili dogovor imperatora Karla IV s gosudarstvennymi činami, *napisannyj* na soroka trex

pergamentnyx listax i *nazvannyj* sim imenem ot
zolotoj pečati, *visjaščej* na černyx i želtyx
šelkovyx snurkax. Na sej pečati izobražen
imperator, *sidjaščij* na trone, s drugoj storony
Rimskaja krepost', ili tak *nazyvaemyj* zamok Sv.
Angela *(il castello di S. Angelo),* s slovami *aurea
Roma* (zolotoj Rim), kotorye *raspoloženy* v trex
linijax takim obrazom:

    aur
    ear
    oma (p. 193)

[In the town hall here, called the Roman
(Römer), they show travelers the hall in which
the newly chosen emperor eats and where there
are hung the portraits of all the emperors from
Konrad I to Karl VI. Whoever does not mind
spending the *červonec* can see in the same
archive the famous 'Golden Bull,' or agreement
between Emperor Karl IV and the ranks of
government which is written on forty-three
parchment pages and which is called by this
name because of its gold seal that hangs on black
and yellow silk cords. On this seal there is
pictured the emperor sitting on the throne and,
on the other side, a Roman fortress, or the so
called Castle of St. Angelo *(il castello di S.
Angelo),* with the words *aurea Roma* (golden
Rome), which are placed in three lines thus:

    aur
    ear
    oma]

As in the case of the adjectives Karamzin chooses, his accumulation of participles tends to emphasize what is observed rather than the observer himself. In her article on Karamzin's use of participles, the contemporary Soviet scholar T. A. Ivanova emphasizes their high frequency in the *Letters* and shows the sharp reduction of the narrator's lyrical presence which results. [19]

Karamzin carefully reflects his interest in objective facts through his choice of syntax. Like his lexical and phraseological choices, his syntax in such descriptions tends toward the impersonal, the factual. V. Stanevich, a contemporary of Karamzin, makes the point that Karamzin's sentence is ordered so as to emphasize his "normal flow of ideas." [20] Given the absence of rhetorical or lyrical considerations, the subject of the sentence ordinarily appears first and is followed by the main verb which is in turn followed by its object, preceded by its modifier. The rest of the predicate then follows. Adjectives immediately precede the nouns they modify; adverbs immediately precede the verbs they modify. Generally adhering to French models, Karamzin economically establishes logical syntactic relationships within the sentence. Even though the average sentence in neutral omniscience tends toward the hypotactic because of the relatively large number of participles, the clause structure is much shorter than was the case with Karamzin's Russian predecessors. In Vinogradov's opinion, Karamzin's logical ordering of the sentence as outlined above both approximated established French word order and accelerated Russian tendencies toward the same syntactic model. [21] Here is a typical example of the sentence in neutral omniscience:

Bernskij aristokratizm počitaetsja samym strožajšim v Švetcarii. Nekotorye familii prisvoil;

sebe vsju vlast' v respublike; iz nix sostavljaetsja
bol'šoj sovet i senat (iz kotoryx pervyj) imeet
zakonodatel'nuju a poslednij — ispolnitel'nuju
vlast'); iz nix vybirajutsja sud'i, tak nazyvaemye
landfoxty, ili praviteli v okrugax, na kotorye
razdelen Bernskij kanton; vse pročie žiteli ne
imejut učastija v pravlenii. (pp. 271-272)

[The Bern aristocracy is considered the strictest
in Switzerland. A few families acquired all the
power in the republic for themselves; they compose the great council and senate (the first has
legislative power while the latter has executive
power). From their number are chosen judges,
the so-called *landvögter* or rulers of the districts
into which the Bern canton is divided; all the
other inhabitants do not have a part in the
government.]

The texture of many nature descriptions is similarly
objective, both in its ordering of the sentence and in word
choice, often tending toward the technical. A presentation
of a waterfall in Switzerland, for example, has all the
pictorial characteristics of a dry topographical survey:

About two *versts* from Lauterbrunnena I saw
the so-called Shtaubbach, or stream which
rushes down from the summit of a stone mountain for nine hundred feet. At this distance it
seems a solid column of milky foam.

With quick steps I drew near to this phenomenon and examined it from all sides. The water
flies straight down, almost without touching the

cliff, and, developing, so to say, in space, falls to the ground in the form of dust or the most delicate silver rain. (p. 256)

Here, Karamzin gives the height of the falls, uses scientific designation "phenomenon," explains from what distance he observed them, and uses bookish clichés ("so to say," "to examine from all sides"). The scene is far removed from the description one might expect from a romantic seeking spiritual communion with Mother Nature. The objectivity of this and other nature descriptions is strikingly different from the lyrical passages which will be discussed later. Here, Karamzin strips his vision of the world to its essential and objective elements, what Čiževskij calls "the sensuous surface of life." [22]

It should not be surprising that Karamzin fills much of his *Letters* with impersonal information about what he observes in the West. As a product of the eighteenth century and its rich legacy of neo-classical thought, Karamzin was quite familiar with a detached, rational attitude toward the physical world. [23] Karamzin was the foremost Russian sentimentalist, but he never ceased to be, in part, a disciple of Enlightenment and some of its attitudes toward external reality. Like his neo-classical predecessors, he at times produces pictorial effects by verbal description incorporating impersonal catalogs of detail that appeal to the eye. These reflect the eighteenth-century poet's aspiration to reproduce in words a sense of visual composition. Positioning by references to right and left, foreground and background, and an almost technical description of color became as important to the poet as they were to the painter. Criticism refers to the union of verbal and visual arts by the term *Ut Pictura Poesis* (as in painting so in poetry). [24] In an aside that shows his own working knowledge of the theory, Karamzin remarks through his narrator, "How many times was it said that visual art cannot compete with poetry? In the representation of *a heart for a heart,* of course; but in everything *pictorial,* for the eye, the poet is the artist's pupil and must tremble when the painter takes his verbal work into his hands." Karamzin's use of the hallowed "speaking pictures" is evident from the following passage describing the environs of Geneva:

> . . . on each elevated place picturesque views open up. The clear expansive Lake Geneva, the Savoy mountain chain behind it shining white, and the villages and small towns scattered along its shore — Morges, Rolle, Nyon — together compose a charming and varied picture. (p. 275)

In this description, as in several others throughout the *Letters,* the size, spatial balance, shape, distance and color of static objects are all of the first importance.

Those sections of the *Letters* that build a profile of the West consistently turn one's attention outward toward objective information, both about the cultural artifacts and customs, and about its varying landscape. There is no sustained lyrical presence. Karamzin's various methods for distinctly separating the fact described from the describer's personality, as discussed above, assure the reader's direct contact with the specifics of foreign life. The narrative mode Karamzin typically chooses for these sections is appropriately, neutral omniscience, for it allows the freest flow of specific facts and is most given to letting those facts "speak for themselves."

In approaching the subjective side of the *Letters* it is important to bear in mind that Karamzin was the first

Russian author to render Western sentimentalism artistically coherent in his country. For much of his life he sought to bring his country into the mainstream of Western intellectual life, with its advanced philosophy, its art, and its progressive esthetics. As literary critic and journalist he consistently directed his efforts toward that goal. He admonished aspiring Russian writers to acquire the "historical information, mental pursuits educated by logic, a subtle taste, and a knowledge of the world" [25] to be found only in Europe. As Karamzin categorically phrased it, a Russian author has the "duty" to "help his countrymen *to think and speak better*" [26] (i.e., as his foreign counterpart had long since learned to do). For him, the guides and teachers to that end were to be found for the Russian author ready-made and available in the West. Karamzin always clung to his firm conviction that Russian authors should serve an apprenticeship and then enter the literary establishment of Europe as an equal partner. "If it is distasteful for us to follow behind others, then we can walk beside them toward the universal goal of humanity. . ." [27] The integration of different national literatures within a single international esthetic is very much a part of Karamzin's concept of progress for Russia. He firmly bound to that concept his view of art as a didactic force to be used by Russian writers in helping the educated Russian to catch up with his more advanced counterpart in the West. [28]

Nowhere is Karamzin's didactic urge to disseminate information of sentimental philosophy and esthetics more integral to his writing than in the *Letters*. His method of propagating the New Sensibility is to be found in the web of digressions he weaves amidst his more objective descriptions. There are basically two variations of the digression. In one, Karamzin adopts a consistently lyrical guise, emphasizing the personal reactions appropriate to a sensitive individual. His responses range from exhilaration to melancholy; events he witnesses excite his memory and private thoughts. He experiences privately what he describes. In other digressions, Karamzin adopts a commenting posture which goes beyond the limits of lyricism. From this position he renders judgments (often abstract and philosophical) about the meaning of what transpires in the *Letters*. He editorializes on what is described, building the digression around reasoned opinion instead of spontaneous feeling. The narrative source (or point of view) for this sort of authorial commentary is editorial omniscience and should be distinguished from the personalized narrator. They nonetheless function jointly to further the didactic program inherent within the travel notes.

As lyrical narrator Karamzin's emotional expressiveness often coincides with one or another sentimental value. As intruding author he just as often delivers a pronouncement *ex cathedra* on that same value, raising it to the level of an abstract principle. The narrator's emotional phrasing thus dovetails with the intruding author's declarative consideration of the same topic. The result is a traditional rhetorical program of instruction based on statement-restatement. The movement goes from particular (emotional) to general (judgmental) and back to particular. The reader's heart and mind are engaged equally by distinct narrative perspectives that, together, familiarize him with a wide range of complementary sentimental issues.

Karamzin's development of his digression system entails the coordination of widely differing genre forms in the *Letters*. These have been noted and partially listed by the Soviet critic T. Roboli (e.g., philosophical discourse, lyrical reveries, short tales, historical and biographical anecdotes, theatrical reviews, translations of foreign literature, etc.) [29] Roboli also traces several of these genres back to separate Western practitioners of the eighteenth century (e.g. the short narratives are reminiscent of those by Gessner and Rousseau; nature descriptions are often patterned after those of Delille. More than random in their appearance, however, Karamzin's use of genre variation represents the core of an integrated didactic plan within the work's subjective sections. Different genres repeat different kinds of sentimental assumptions and proceed from different narrative sources (i.e., the narrator and the intruding author). Distinguishing between those genres and the narrative modes governing them reveals the architecture of Karamzin's instructive program.

On one hand Karamzin addresses his readers in a number of genre forms that demand rational understanding and thoughtful consideration. These include intellectual digressions by Karamzin as commenting author (what Roboli calls authorial discourse), synopses of prominent Western philosophical systems of the day, and analyses of critical theories of the drama. The narrative perspective in each case is editorial omniscience. On the other hand, Karamzin frequently appeals to his readers' emotions in the form of lyrical digressions, short narrations and anecdotes, and in his selection of literary quotes together with his private responses to them. In each of these cases Karamzin speaks as a personalized narrator whose feelings about what he describes are consistently conspicuous. Karamzin, when he speaks through editorial omniscience, is thoroughly intellectual and calls on the reader to respond on a conceptual level to what he says. As narrator, Karamzin is emotionally effusive and consistently calls forth the reader's own emotional potential to mingle with his own. Karamzin's shifting from one narrative perspective to the other throughout the *Letters* creates the effect of a carefully developed structure which both posits and reinforces key sentimental values.

On the level of Karamzin's editorial omniscience the intellectual digressions are central to this design. It is here that Karamzin's text directly calls for the reader's studied reflection and for agreement with sentimental principles, stated in their most concise form. For example:

> Our life is divided into two epochs: the first we pass in the future and the second in the past. Up to a certain age, man, in the pride of his hopes, looks always forward with the thought: 'There, there awaits me a fate worthy of my heart!' Losses grieve him but little, the future seems to him to be an inexhaustible coffer, prepared for his pleasure. But when the fever of youth passes, when self respect, insulted for the hundredth time, unwillingly learns acquiescence, when, deluded by hope for the hundredth time, we finally cease to believe in it, then, relinquishing the future with sorrow, we turn our eyes to the past and wish to exchange the lost happiness of seductive expectations for pleasant memories, saying to ourselves: 'And we, and we were in Arcadia!'
>
> (p. 554)

The sentimental *topoi* used here are "false hopes held by the young" and "nostalgia for a better past." Both articulate on the question of melancholy. In the eighteenth century such themes were common stock in the poetry of Gray, Thomson and Macpherson, to mention just a few. It is important, however, to observe how Karamzin selects his style and arranges his material. He appeals specifically to the conceptual faculties of his reader, maintaining a generalized tone with the aphoristic formula: "Our life is divided into two epochs:. . . ." The hypotaxis beginning with: "But when the fever. . . ," imitates the logician's statement of a proposition with its incremental series of clauses beginning with "when," followed by a series of answering clauses beginning with "then."

In another of his intellectual digressions, Karamzin emphasizes a different important sentimental *topos,* the concept of man's complex personality and the ways in which it manifests itself — in individuality and variation:

> *Temperament* is the basis of our moral being, while *character* is its accidental form. We are born with a temperament, but without character, which is formed little by little from external influences. The character depends, of course, on the temperament, but only in part, depending, among other things, on the kind of objects that act on us. The unique ability to accept influences is the temperament; the form, which these impressions give to the moral being, is character. A single object produces various responses in people — why? From the variety of temperaments or from the different characteristics of the *moral mass* which is a child.
>
> (pp. 282-283)

Again, Karamzin matches the abstract and generalized quality of his idea with a style that demands the reader's reasoning capacities. He makes of the passage a reasoned explanation, a definition of the principle of individualism rather than an example of it.

Nature's superiority over man's prideful production

of art, a prominent feature of Rousseau's philosophy, is reserved for another digression:

> What do all our vaults mean before the vault of heaven? How much intellect and physical labors are required to make such a lowly production. Is not art the most shameless ape of nature when it seeks to compete with it in grandeur!
>
> (p. 542)

Like the first examples, this digression is marked by a formal style. Karamzin expands rhetorical questions into a syntactic focus; he generalizes to mankind as a whole. He relies on balanced clauses to reinforce the idea he develops, and resorts to striking juxtapositions of size and quality to drive those ideas home. Karamzin, as commenting author, takes on the role of lecturer; the reader's role is that of an attentive student whose task it is to absorb the aphoristic lesson. Similarly abstract preachments on the moral superiortiy of the past over the present, or the idea that nature is man's best guide in life appear in other digressions and are characterized by the same declarative style.

Karamzin's auctorial digressions serve as key reference points in the *Letters,* both by their introduction of sentimental principles, and by their compressed expression. In other places, however, he varies the work's instructive design by quoting the thoughts and writings of important contemporary philosophers sympathetic to sentimental ideas (e.g., Kant, Baumgarten, Lavater, Herder, Gellert and others). The opinions of such luminaries generally complement the values found in the intruding author's own digressions. For example, Karamzin's digressions about individualism and variability among people are supported by Karamzin's quotation of Lavater's own ideas on the subject. The well-known moral philosopher and phrenologist presents a compact apology for each person's searching out his own means of approaching eternal laws of self-awareness (which Lavater associates with the development of a growing moral sense). Karamzin quotes him as follows:

> Being is the goal of being. Feeling and the happiness of being *(Daseynsfrohheit)* is the goal of everything that we can seek. The wise and the weak-minded seek only the means of enjoying their own being or feeling it. They seek that through which they can feel their own existence more strongly. Each *feeling* and each *thing* perceived by any of our feelings is an addition *(Beyträge)* to our self-consciousness *(Selbstgefühles)*. The more self-consciousness, the more pleasure. Just as our constitutions and educations are different, so different also are our needs in *means* and *objects* which allow us to feel in a new way our being, our strengths, our life. The wise man differs from the weak-minded only in his methods of self-consciousness.
>
> (p. 240)

The compressed thought stands apart from surrounding passages of description. As is the case in Karamzin's own digressions or related topics, this passage is abstract and seeks to emphasize the general applicability of its dominant idea, relying on syntactic repetitions to enhance its message.

Karamzin's introduction of sentimental philosophers and synopses of their key ideas is extensive. For example, he refers to Baumgarten, the early eighteenth-century German pioneer of esthetics as a science, by emphasizing the German's theoretical association between a sense of beauty and the personal feelings of the viewer. Karamzin thereby reinforces his own oft-repeated emphasis on subjectivity. A number of philosophers are discussed who raise the sentimental issue of overcoming death by adhering to the eternal strength of morality. Kant ruminates on man's frustrations and lack of fulfillment in this life, projecting that goal into the better existence that lies beyond the grave. Kant insists that one's moral acts, prompted by private conscience, forms his sole comfort as he looks back over his life on earth. His moral sensitivity helps man recognize and look forward to the better existence to come. Herder is quoted as reinforcing the same optimism in his meditation on nature's perennial triumph of spring over winter. Karamzin quotes Herder's thoughts in which the German compares that hopeful event in nature with man's struggle to find meaning in his own inevitable death:

> And so there is no death in creation; or death is nothing else but *the removal of that which can no longer be,* that is *the action of a perpetually young, tireless power* which, by its properties, cannot be wasteful or rest for a single moment. In accordance with the beautiful law of wisdom and grace, everything strives toward the new strength of youth and beauty — it strives and changes at every moment.
>
> (p. 173)

Again, the passage Karamzin chooses is characterized by an analytical, declarative tone in which the author often resorts to definitions (a quality equally evident in Karamzin's own digressions). Karamzin includes the moral philosopher Gellert's thoughts by way of his anonymous biographer whose words echo the same association of immortality and morality, so important in sentimentalism's hierarchy of values.

Karamzin is careful to select the weighty pronouncements of philosophers close to the doctrines of sensibility. Their reputations, the fact that their words appear in quoted form, the abstract phrasing of their ideas, all lend an aura of authority to the catalog of lessons he teaches in the *Letters*. It is ironically apt that Descartes, the neo-classical idol of rationalism, is mentioned only in passing, and then as a negative example. Karamzin refers to the great materialist as being so bound to a mechanistic view of the world that something as spiritual and abstract as a nightingale's song threatened his entire rational scheme (p. 543).

As intruding author Karamzin augments his reader's intellectual grasp of sentimental values by presenting theoretical discussions of both neo-classical and sentimental literary esthetics. In the process he indicates clearly his preference for the latter. Of central importance to the present discussion is the fact that he explains why he so chooses. He thus turns those sections of the *Letters* into an ordered series of reasoned explanations and justifications of sentimental beliefs that border on lectures. Karamzin was extremely well read and his considered opinions on the competing literary schools of his time are still valuable for their insights into Europe's transition in taste to the New Sensibility.

Of particular interest here are Karamzin's theoretical discussions of contrasting theories of the drama. He compares the French neo-classical tradition with the new, emotion-centered taste that favored Shakespeare. By juxta-posing the two esthetic theories of drama and explaining his principles that favor Shakespeare, as he was understood by the *Sturm und Drang* movement, Karamzin expands the reader's theoretical familiarity with Western sentimental taste. He flatly rejects the neo-classical tendency to ver-balize important events and psychological states of mind through long monologs maintaining that such an approach vitiates the emotional involvement of the audience (p. 353). Repeating his objection to French tragedy in a later entry he demands a pathetic emphasis in the theatre, the presentation of feeling "to deeply stir our hearts or horrify the soul" (p. 390). To complete his explanation of what makes for great drama he gives a short analysis of Shakes-peare's *King Lear,* emphasizing the presence of exactly what French tragedy lacks — the exhibition of strong emotion on stage, freed from any rational symmetry and elegant phrasing. Shakespeare's verses "lacerate the soul; they rumble like the thunder which is described in them and shake the reader's soul" (p. 391). Here, as in other digressions appearing in editorial omniscience, Karamzin adopts a declarative tone which proceeds from the judg-ment of detached authority.

Whether it be his own gnomic pronouncements, his discussion of philosophers sympathetic to those values, or his theoretical definitions of good drama, Karamzin builds a persuasive, essentially conceptual presentation of senti-mental taste. Such digressive moments form a single system of their own within the *Letters,* distinct from the neutral omniscient passages of description that surround each of them. The digressions are stylistically united in their vigorous appeal to the reader's powers of abstract thinking, their avoidance of emotional coloration, and their generalized application.

Karamzin's direct analyses of sentimental concepts function in unison with an equally well-integrated system of indirect supports for those same ideals. Assuming the voice of "narrator-as-observer" in these digressions he emphasizes subjective lyricism rather than reasoned abstractions. The reader's intellectual grasp of sentimental canons here turns to a personal sense of identification with the narrator's intimate personality. The categories of indirect instruction include the narrator's numerous lyrical pauses, his use of secondary narrations, and his introduction of literary quotes and references from important sentimental pieces of literature.

Approaching Karamzin's lyrical digressions, for example, one is struck by how thoroughly he restates in emotional terms what he clearly reasons out in his intellectual digressions. For instance, the central sentimental idea of melancholy contemplation of this life, which finds expression in the intruding author's words on page 554, is given a more emotional phrasing on page 401:

> Why does my heart sometimes suffer without any known reason? Why does the light darken in my eyes when the bright sun shines in the sky? How am I to explain these cruel melancholy attacks during which my whole soul contracts and grows cold? . . Can this sorrow be a portent of distant calamities? Can it be none other than an advance on those heartaches with which fate is intending to visit me in the future?

Vague expectations of sorrow, frustration and eventual calamity, all point to the same lesson which Karamzin explains theoretically — that man must put aside false optimism and recognize how life's hopes are bound to fall short of fulfillment.

Moving to a related sentimental preoccupation — optimism toward life after the grave as a means of enduring the frustration of this life — Karamzin again provides complementary intellectual and lyrical expressions of the same theme. I have already discussed his clear invocation of Kant, Herder and Lavater to emphasize his own hopeful vision on this point. In a lyrical rephrasing of the same idea, he ecstatically professes a deeply personal faith in that better existence to come:

> Ach! If I had to die now, at this very minute, I
> would drop into the all-embracing lap of nature
> with a tear of love, with full confidence that it is
> calling me to happiness, that the transformation
> of my being is a heightening of beauty, an
> exchange of the beautiful for something better.
> And always, my dear friends, always when in
> spirit I return to the pristine simplicity of
> human nature, when my heart opens out toward
> the beauties of nature — I feel the same and find
> nothing fearsome in death.
>
> (p. 215)

Rousseau's principle, that nature affects man's attitudes and personality, is prominent in several digressions that appear in editorial omniscience. Karamzin varies and strengthens that idea with a number of complementary lyrical pauses. For example, the quick paling of color in nature at sundown reminds him of life's transitoriness: " So passes the glory of the world! So wilts the rose of youth! So dies the lamp of life! " (p. 251). Lyrical comparisons of nature's seasons with the stages of man's life are especially common to sentimentalist writers (e.g., Thomson's *The Seasons*). Karamzin draws on the convention throughout the *Letters:* "Autumn makes me a melancholiac. . . sadness mixes in my heart with a kind of sweet contentment. Ach! I have never felt so vitally that the flow of nature is the image of our own life's flow! . . Where are you, spring of my life? Quickly, quickly passes the summer — and at this moment my heart feels autumn's chill. Farewell my friends!" (pp. 296-297).

The numerous anecdotes and short narratives which Karamzin-as-narrator introduces into the *Letters* are most important in the work's emotional program. Like his own lyrical digressions, his cameo-like narrative inserts resonate to specific sentimental values. The emotional potential of these short narratives is enriched by devices that appeal to the reader's emotions such as direct quotations of characters' speeches, descriptions of characters' feelings during moments of emotional stress, and rudimentary symbolism. In addition, the narrator is involved in the tales through his own lyrical reaction to the events he describes.

One of Karamzin's last entries (on page 599) provides a simple case in point. On his way home by ship, the captain tells the narrator a story about a passenger he once had on board. The passenger, Maria V., had to leave a secret suitor in London to follow her father to America. The father subsequently died. Having fulfilled her duty as a daughter, she was free to return to her home and her waiting betrothed. During the ocean passage she fell ill and despaired of ever seeing her lover again. She died, pathetically hallucinating that she was in England, happy in her lover's arms. The narrator identifies strongly with the girl and thinks of her burial at sea in terms of himself:

"Imagine, they threw the poor thing into the sea! Imagine, I sleep on her bed! . . . 'So you would throw me into the sea if I were to die on your ship?' I asked the captain. 'What could I do?' he answered with a shrug of his shoulders. This is horrible!" Inspired by the somber mood of his own story the narrator ruminates on the inevitability of his own future death: "Earth, earth! Prepare a secluded place in your quiet depths for my dust!" As brief and simple as the narrative piece is, it is carefully designed to arouse emotions (fear, pity, admiration, anger). Reinforced by these emotions, the short tale serves the function of restating, in varied form, the familiar attitude of melancholy pessimism that takes so many different shapes within the work.

The prominent sentimental point of fate's destruction of hope in this life appears in a number of similar narrative inserts. In one Karamzin describes the pathetic deaths of two lovers (on page 335). An ideal, virtuous couple, they await their marriage among a group of happy friends. In an excess of excitement, the bride ventures too close to a precipice and falls to her death. Suffering terribly from his shock, the groom cannot bear his loss and falls dead on the spot. The parents of the lovers grieve until their own deaths. Karamzin saturates the narrative with vigorous emotional appeals. As the responsive narrator he underscores his feeling for the lovers, calling them "gentle Jean" and "dear Lizaveta." He recreates their cries of lament, their shock at seeing sudden death in all its immediacy. Karamzin heightens the scene's emotional impact by introducing a jarring succession of paratactic clauses that convey the narrator's sense of personal involvement with each stage of Lizaveta's fall and death: "She gasped — tried to grab onto something but had no time — the mountain was shaking — everything was tumbling — the unfortunate girl plunged into the abyss, and perished!" The same syntactic ordering carries the hero's equally pathetic end: "Jean wanted to throw himself after her — his legs failed him — he fell senseless to the ground." The narrator transposes himself into the position of discovering Jean's death in a series of syntactic bursts: ". . . they laid a hand to his heart — it was not beating — Jean had died!" Throughout, the syntax Karamzin chooses evokes the impression of personal involvement with what is described. He heightens the incident's traumatic value by his narrator's remark "my heart shudders."

The theme of fate destroying hope in this life appears in a number of Karamzin's inserted tales. In another, star-crossed lovers, along with their happy guests, set out to row on a beautifully placid lake (symbolic of their happy expectations of life) only to be caught unawares in a sudden storm (fate's appearance in its hostility). All the members of the party can do is "wipe away the last tear shed for life" and drown. The infection of pessimism touches Karamzin's fictionalized narrator as it so often does: "With sorrowing thoughts I pondered this castle [the lovers' home] ; the wind blew from its deserted walls" (p. 255).

It is characteristic of Karamzin's use of these short narratives that their *personae* appear only in terms of their strong emotion (e.g., the quick movement from happy optimism to unanswerable shock and sorrow, helpless pathos, or lingering grief). No character has any dimension to his personality outside these emotions. They serve primarily as vehicles for enhancing the overall suggestion of crushed hope and its melancholy aftermath. The resultant mood thus reinforces Karamzin's own treatments of pessimism and melancholy in his role as both lyrical narrator and intruding author.

While most of the short tales come from Karamzin's narrator himself, some are related by episodic characters whom he meets during his travels. It is in keeping with the overall pattern of the *Letters* that this variation of the narrative insert also supports basic sentimental doctrines advanced elsewhere in the work. Like a wheel within a wheel, one narrator introduces the reader to a second narrator. The emotional vigor of a stranger infects the primary narrator who in turn amplifies the mood as he conveys it to his reader. For example, the narrator meets an old invalid soldier who wistfully remembers a better time, saying it was superior to the present (on pages 331-332). An abbot decries the materialist value system of contemporary society and looks back upon a golden age that was free of worldly pursuits (on pages 379-380). At another point in his travels, the narrator encounters a female version of Ossian who lives in a deserted, mysterious castle. She also laments the passing of a way of life more noble than the dissolute present (on pages 402-403).

Such narratives from secondary sources as those above share a debt to Macpherson and his type of sentimental fascination with moral superiority of the dim past. Here also are the characteristic emotive devices Karamzin's narrator uses in his own recounted tales. Direct rendering of dialog, moody nature descriptions, the narrator's emphasis on the virtues of the heroes, and numerous emotional exclamations, all help to enlist the reader's sympathy for the idea inherent in each of the tales, as they do in the central narrator's own vignettes. Nor does Karamzin let a chance go by to let the sad events, described by someone else, mingle with his own lyrical response. After the poor old woman has finished her sad tale (pages 402-403), Karamzin caps the moment with the spontaneous thought: "My God! How much magnificence there is in the physical world, — I thought, — and how much misfortune in the spiritual! Can an unfortunate [person], weighed down with the burden of his existence, rejected and alone among multitudes of cold and cruel people, — can he rejoice in your grandeur, golden sun!''

Karamzin is at times given to sharing his favorite pieces of fiction with the reader. These are usually Western masterpieces which exemplify issues of emotional expressiveness. Just as the intruding author's numerous references to philosophers and their systems of thought are intended to reinforce the reader's intellectual grasp of sentimental ideals, so does the narrator's repeated quotation from important sentimental works reinforce emotional familiarity with those same values. For example, the narrator lingers over some of the emotional high points of Sterne's *Sentimental Journey,* mingling his own innermost feelings with those he describes in Sterne's book. The emotional value of the scene is thereby enhanced and his Russian reader's knowledge of the English sentimentalist's work is made more firm. The narrator recounts his visit to the island of St. Pierre on which Rousseau composed *Promenades Solitaires* and relishes his sense of kinship with the Frenchman. He is stirred to the point of entering into the same contemplation of a better world that lies beyond death which affected Rousseau's work. As the narrator personally assures his readers, such was Rousseau's only alternative to the haunting pessimism that affected his own life. One of St. Preux's letters to Julie, full of pessimism and sorrow over their separation, appears in quoted form on pages 278-279. The omnipresent motif of melancholy finds another variation in Karamzin's reference to the opera *Atisa.* He praises one of its arias "Vivre ou mourir" in which two lovers share their sense of persecution at the hands of fate and Cybele (p. 292). An ode by Addison stresses a pietistic hymn of praise for true friendship. Shakespeare speaks of the greater value of one's inner nobility over mere material possessions. Haller's idyll "Die Alpen" praises the peasants' happiness in nature which even the wealthiest kings must envy. Both authors function here to exemplify the principle of turning away from society's idols to search for life's spiritual meaning.

By peppering his notes with the names of important sentimental authors and recounting snatches of their best-known works, Karamzin maintains the didactic scheme of his *Letters.* Macpherson's *Fingal,* Goldsmith's *The Vicar of Wakefield,* Richardson's *Clarissa* and *Pamela,* Schiller's tragedy *Fiesko* (full of the same strong feeling which Karamzin recommends in his more abstract critical analysis of Shakespeare), Goethe's *Sorrows of Young Werther,* Thomson's *The Seasons,* Gray's "Elegy in a Country Churchyard," Rousseau's *La Nouvelle Héloïse,* are a few of the many significant works of sentimentalism that find their way into the *Letters* via the narrator's lyrical musings and associations. The sheer weight of Karamzin's references to such works and their central themes provided a highly educative service to the Russian reader who was still impatiently trying to absorb the ethos of cultivated sentiment.

Occasionally Karamzin's narrator expands his normally capsulized reference to contemporary literature to recount the entire plot of one or another piece. Here, as in the more numerous short quotes and references, a theme typical of some central sentimental value dominates the reader's attention and evokes an appropriate emotional response from the narrator. For example, he describes a French melodrama *(Peter the Great)* which concerns the Tsar's fictionalized marriage to a peasant girl in a foreign country "not far from Russia's borders." Disguising himself as a simple workman, he is learning the country's skills in shipbuilding. When Peter meets an especially attractive country lass he gives free reign to his spontaneous heart and proposes to her, all the while retaining the secret of his identity. His aide, also in disguise, sounds the work's sentimental theme of spiritual equality between representatives of different social classes in his address to Peter: ". . . you are great of soul; you wish to raise the dignity of man in our country and despise the vain arrogance of others; nobility of the soul alone is worthy of respect in your eyes; Catherine is noble in her soul — and so let her be the wife of my lord, my father and my friend!" (p. 397). Forced to leave his betrothed because of a mutiny in Russia, he later returns to reveal his true identity to Catherine, explaining his disguise with the words: "I wished to possess a tender heart. . . which would love in me, not the emperor, but the man: here is that heart! My heart and hand are yours; accept them and the crown from me! The crown will not grace you, but you it" (p. 399). The substitution of spiritual excellence for social class as the central basis for personal familiarity is a basic sentimental assumption. Here it is played out twice: once between Peter and his aide (who looks on the Tsar more as a friend than an absolute master) and once between Peter and the peasant girl. That principle's appearance in story form, replete with emotional props, indirectly repeats and strengthens the idea by acting it out. The narrator openly partakes of the theme's interest. Dispersed throughout his synopsis of the play are remarks like "Imagine the Tsar's sensitivity!" or "I wipe away my tears and rejoice that I am a Russian." Theme, characters' quoted speech, the narrator's own responses, all unite to support the same sentimental consideration.

The great value of *Letters of a Russian Traveler* lies in Karamzin's talent to sum up a whole era in Western thought and esthetics. The work represents an incisive analysis of exactly what was going on in the intellectual life of the countries whose cultural taste played such a formative role in Russia's growth towards membership in the European community. One part of the *Letters* presents a veritable encyclopedia of specific information about Western manners, places and institutions. Here Karamzin satisfied the educated Russian's hunger for knowledge he had little chance of acquiring first-hand. In such sections Karamzin consistently chooses neutral omniscience as the most appropriate narrative mode for his purpose.

An equally educative program also unifies the digressive sections of the *Letters.* It is a different kind of education than the objective facts of names and places. But it fulfilled the Russian's equally strong desire for initiation into the central beliefs of sentimentalism which had come to dictate his reading habits and his changing vision of himself. Karamzin's method of familiarizing his countrymen with the new taste is an intricate and beautifully balanced one. Based on a combination of narrative perspectives, Karamzin develops traditional rhetorical models through which he appeals to the reader's intellectual and emotional faculties. What he states clearly in the form of a compressed principle (in editorial omniscience) he is more than likely to restate in the form of his narrator's lyrical expressiveness. Sober philosophical analyses of sentimental values, propounded by authorities like Kant or Baumgarten, have a distinct tendency to reappear in the more emotional form of abbreviated tales tucked away between the narrator's visit to museums. Theoretical discussions about the merits of exhibited passion in drama come alive in the narrator's description and personal reaction to *King Lear, Fiesko,* or *Peter the Great.* Throughout, Karamzin keeps important sentimental authors, themes, and titles before his reader's eyes. Throughout, his balanced appeals to the reader's heart and mind gradually ease him into familiarity with Europe's philosophy of feeling. Karamzin's choice of different narrative voices to accommodate different presentations of those lessons bears testimony to the care with which he executed his didactic program.

The *Letters* conforms to Karamzin's general purpose behind publishing the *Moscow Journal* in the early 1790s and it was in that journal that the notes began to appear. Both enterprises are most clearly appreciated as means of exposing the educated Russian to the more sophisticated cultural phenomena of Western Europe. As an educational piece, the *Letters* accelerated and clarified those principles of sentimentalism that so fascinated Russian readers.

The narrative perspective of editorial omniscience that Karamzin develops so extensively in the *Letters* is not substantially different from the function of editor in the *Journal.* In both cases Karamzin inspired the reader to understand and appreciate the West's established sensibility. The *Letters* thus accomplished in microcosm what the *Journal* sought to achieve on a larger scale — the integration of original Russian prose and poetry, with *precis* of foreign literature together with criticism and reviews of its drama, all cemented together with essays on events and people who affect the literary scene. [30]

The impression Karamzin creates in his travel notes is a doubly optimistic one. His compositional emphasis on teaching his Russian readers the good news of sentimentalism assumes that they would be able to learn it. As well, there are no problems left unsolved in Karamzin's balancing of sentimental considerations about life and its meaning. The haunting frustrations of disappointment in man's existence, so often present in the *Letters,* are usually resolved through the rejuvenating powers of an afterlife. Sorrow is made tolerable by the warmth of friends and the untiring forces of nature. The almost omnipresent theme of man's finitude is answered by Kant's and Lavater's faith in perpetual harmony to come after death. The artificiality of modern, complex society does not smother the sensitive individual's ability to refresh himself in his imagination and in his communion with moral ideals.

The world of feeling that Karamzin presents is a stable one, ruled over by principles that find clear formulation in editorial omniscience. The intruding author controls the reader's thoughts, pointing him to answers when serious questions arise. Karamzin also poses and resolves those questions in emotional terms, through this narrator, in an equally systematic and controlled manner. For Karamzin, the moral and esthetic system of sentimentalism poses an alternative to the capricious "reality" that weighs so on the man of sensibility. The role of proselytizer that he assumes in the *Letters* bespeaks his faith that Russians could appreciate that alternative and participate in it as the West had already learned to do.

2

The First Group of Tales:

Optimism Affirmed

The education in sentimental values inherent in the *Letters* figures prominently in Karamzin's general activity with the *Moscow Journal* (e.g., in his choice of translations and reviews of foreign sentimental works). That same design is similarly characteristic of many of the prose tales he composed and published in its issues (e.g., "Poor Liza," "Natalia the Boyar's Daughter," "The Beautiful Princess and the Fortunate Dwarf"). "Julia," which also bears evidence of Karamzin's sentimental didacticism and is considered here to belong to this group, was written later and appeared separately.

These tales are readily distinguishable one from the other in terms of their genre designations and their tone varies from melancholy to tongue-in-cheek humor to ringing seriousness. Despite those dissimilarities, however, they are yet united in their shared propagation of important assumptions of the New Sensibility (e.g., personal morality, sad disappointment, true love overcoming social barriers, natural education, the sanctity of the home, the superiority of the country over the city, etc.).

The didactic impulse of each tale is largely realized by the narrative method Karamzin adopts in it. As in the *Letters*, he at times resorts to direct authorial discourse with the reader (i.e., editorial omniscience). Through this mode Karamzin provides himself with a superior perspective from which to deliver judgments on his characters and to call on the reader for his reasoned agreement with those judgments. At other moments he presents himself as a narrator *persona* with all the limitations of an experiencing and feeling personality. As narrator he often elicits an emotional reaction from the reader concerning a character or an event. At other times he dons the guise to provide the aura of verisimilitude in the recounting of certain details he supposedly witnessed. As in the *Letters*, it is important to distinguish adequately between the two "voices" — the intruding author and the narrator — that Karamzin assumes as he organizes his fabula material. What superficially appears to be the presence of simply the "ego form" within the narrative flow is not a single entity but is divisible. Each voice has its own consistent properties and its own function as an interpretive force within the work. As will be pointed out, Karamzin's choice of the narrator *persona*, which is extremely prominent structurally in "Poor Liza," is almost absent from succeeding tales in this group. The reasons for both the narrator's presence and its absence, and its role as coordinated with Karamzin's use of the intruding author, are important to an understanding of the wide variation in effect among these early tales.

"POOR LIZA"

"Bednaja Liza" ["Poor Liza"] (1791) is

Karamzin's first tale after his return from abroad. It is his most famous work of fiction and its appearance in Russian and Western anthologies has traditionally (but unfairly) determined the general reader's acquaintance with the author. Its impact on Karamzin's contemporaries can hardly be imagined today. Dmitrii Blagoy, in his history of Russian literature, gives an idea of its importance when he declares it to be the single most important piece of sentimental prose in Russia. [1] Its popularity as the most influential story in Russia was unchallenged for several years after its appearance. [2]

The story concerns a young peasant girl (Liza) and her chaste love for a handsome but jaded young man of the gentry class (Erast). Liza meets him and falls in love when she comes to Moscow to sell flowers. Her purity and charm fascinate Erast who sees in her a chance to partake, at least for a while, of the innocence and simplicity so absent from his city-bred ways. Their love is at first idyllic, cast against the Arcadian country setting of Moscow's environs. Even though their different social backgrounds make marriage impossible, they continue their secret meetings with the inevitable result of a physical consummation to their love. Liza's devotion to Erast is now irreversible and Erast's interest wanes, since his adventure can go no further. Military obligations soon carry him away and into marriage with a rich older woman whom he does not love. Later, Liza accidentally meets Erast in Moscow and learns of her lover's betrayal. Shamed by his present of one hundred rubles and his order to the servants to remove Liza from the house, she loses all sense of purpose in life and drowns herself. Erast grieves for the rest of his life, realizing his responsibility for Liza's death, and gives up all hope of finding again the love Liza had offered him.

The bare thematic outline of the tale is a conventional one for eighteenth-century Europe.[3] Karamzin's handling of the familiar theme is what created its huge success in Russia. For one thing, Karamzin condenses the events into short story form rather than relying on Richardson's ponderous novels (e.g., *Pamela* 1740, Goethe's *The Trials of Young Werther* 1774, or the derivative prose of Karamzin's countryman L'vov *(Russkaja Pamela [A Russian Pamela]* 1789). Earlier Russian novels on the same subject, with their chains of wandering encounters, epistolary confessions and love entanglements, seem needlessly bulky in comparison with Karamzin's fast pace and well-defined denouement. The swiftness and clarity with which Karamzin moves from idyllic love to the crucial error of physical intercourse to the tragic finale of Liza's suicide and Erast's unremitting guilt altogether captured the Russian reader's attention as no earlier piece of national fiction.

Karamzin graces his story with a number of the more potent esthetic and philosophical tenets of sentimentalism. Many represent a continuation of those principles found in the *Letters,* but with an important structural difference. In the *Letters* he strung together a series of loosely-organized episodes based on his travels; each episode usually illustrated a single sentimental consideration. In "Poor Liza" he more tightly organizes a select number of those values and integrates them into a single *fabula*. His task is an intensive one rather than extensive as compared with the travel notes.

The narrator of "Poor Liza" is not unlike Karamzin's traveler in the *Letters* in that they are both one step removed from the events and characters they describe. Each narrator is a structured and recognizable personality in the work, subject to human limits of thought and feeling. Each represents himself as involved in the events of the work but, although each commiserates or rejoices with the various characters he describes, neither becomes an active participant. They both stand to one side, conveying what happens and describing their personal responses to those events.

The lyrical side of Karamzin's narrator in "Poor Liza" is the key to the tale's enormous affective quality and entails a number of the West's most hallowed sentimental ideals. For example, Karamzin cultivates the aura of verisimilitude particularly through his narrator. He represents himself as a believable person who renders an account of "actual" people. Events occur in a recognizable place, not far from where the reader might well live. The success of that illusion is proven by the many pilgrimages undertaken by sympathetic Russian readers who thought they could tell exactly where Liza's cottage was and where the pond was located in which she drowned herself.[4] The narrator assures his "friend" the reader that both places are but a short distance from Moscow. Her home is "some seventy *sazhens* from the walls of the Se-nov Monastery gates, by a stand of birch in the middle of a green meadow."[5] The cottage's ramshackle appearance, which he minutely describes, marks her residence for the curious. He assures the reader of his thorough familiarity with the place which can easily be seen from the Moscow River below.

The novelty of a personalized "I" telling the story who had actually met a principal character (he says Erast himself told him the story years after the events had taken place) and who had "verified" his information about the people he describes, caused a literary sensation in Russia. Karamzin's guise of authenticity serves two related purposes. First, the narrator's knowledge of the locale and

his contact with Erast allow Karamzin to present a great
deal of unquestioned fact in the story and thereby draw
the reader into the illusion of verisimilitude. The narrator
answered the popular wish of that time to engage the
reader in the lives of particular individuals, to provide a
feeling of knowing all about their lives. The wealth of
detail concerning various physical settings, together with
summaries of fabula events which he supplies, provide a
rich basis for reader participation in the tale.

Karamzin's second and related use of the narrator's
authenticity is to justify the inclusion of personal thoughts
and feelings in many sections of the story. In these
sections Karamzin superimposes an emotional consciousness onto the "factual" settings and reported events of the
tale. Through the prominent narrator, he thereby controls
and directs the reader's emotional perception of the fabula
events. As narrator he intertwines his own personality with
described events so as to make them flow into one
another. The effect is that, in addition to feeling that he is
watching real people, the reader becomes emotionally
involved in their lives. For example, when Liza is thinking
about the handsome Erast early in the story he suddenly
appears before her. The narrator becomes caught up in the
psychological thrill that Liza experiences and amplifies her
feeling with his own reaction:

> But Liza, Liza stood with downcast gaze, with
> fiery cheeks, with trembling heart — she could
> not take her hand away from his — she could
> not turn away when he drew close to her with
> his pink lips . . . Ach! He kissed her, kissed her
> with such ardor that the whole world seemed to
> be ablaze!

As narrator, Karamzin strengthens the impression of his spontaneous reaction to the situation by adopting a rhythm in his language, stringing together successive exclamatory, almost breathless clauses. He also enhances the scene's emotional effect by making the clauses of equal length, organizing each around repeated key words. The fact that he indulges in heat imagery to emphasize the heroine's inner tension further emphasizes the impression of emotional excitation in the scene which applies to character and narrator alike.

The narrator directs questions to his heroine that convey his personal concern about her state of mind. He worries over her love affair with Erast and generally involves himself in her fate. Given the traditional nature of the narrator device, the reader identifies his own sympathies with those of the personalized teller, allowing himself to be directed by his keen emotional involvement with Liza and Erast. He, like his "friend" the narrator is apprehensive over Liza's lovelorn state: "Ach, Liza, Liza! What has happened to you . . . " His agitation at times makes it impossible to continue his narrative. When Liza and Erast declare their love for one another he exclaims: "she could hardly believe her own ears and . . . But I throw away my brush." When he describes the passionate consumation of their love, the narrator's agitation comes through clearly in his hasty piling up of short clauses built around key repeated words:

> Erast felt an unusual agitation in his blood — never had Liza seemed so charming to him — never had her caresses affected him so strongly — never had her kisses been so fiery — she knew nothing, suspected nothing, feared nothing . . .

Like a coda at the end of a repeated motif he exclaims "Ach, Liza, Liza! Where is your guardian angel? Where – is your innocence?"

When the full extent of Erast's rejection of Liza is revealed to her, the narrator lives the moment with the heroine, reflecting her surprise, shock, and anger in his own words:

> My heart bleeds at this moment. I forget the man in Erast – I am ready to damn him – But my tongue does not move – I look at the sky and a tear rolls down my face. Ach! Why am I not writing a novel rather than a sad true tale?

In addition to his overt involvement with specific events in the tale, the narrator generates an appropriately melancholy mood before Liza's story begins and after it ends. Karamzin creates the lyrical frame by plaiting the narrator's feelings with external "reality." Here, it is objects and nature, rather than events, which serve Karamzin's emotive purpose. The suggestive texture of physical descriptions enhances the aura of doom and sorrow which hangs over the tale.

The monastery, which serves a landmark for finding Liza's home, evokes associations of death and lost hope in the narrator. He imagines an old monk who has nothing to look forward to in life. Then his imagination runs to the image of a young monk in the same monastery who yearns to be free but who is doomed to solitary silence. The sense of sad decay shrouding the monastery, complete with grave stones and a mournful wind, dominates his thinking process. His language reflects the same sadness by the suggestive repetition of back vowels which match the sound of the wind:

Strašno vojut vetry v stenax opustevšego monastyrja, meždu grobov, zarosšix vysokoju travoju, i v temnyx perexodax kelij. Tam, opersis' na razvaliny grobnyx kamnej, vnimaju gluxomu stonu, bezdnoju minuvšego pogloš-čennyj, — stonu, ot kotorogo serdce moe sodrogaetsja i trepešcet.

[the winds howl fearfully among the walls of the deserted monastery, amidst the graves grown up with tall grass, and in the dark passageways of the cells. There, leaning on the ruins of the grave stones I listen to a hollow groan, engulfed by the abyss of the past. It is a groan that makes my heart contract and tremble.]

From there his lyrical impressions move to more general thoughts about mournful moments in Russia's history (i.e., its occupation by Lithuanian and Tatar forces) as a means of expanding on his own personal melancholy.

Ruminations on broken hope and static disappointment set the mood for Karamzin's recounting of Liza's equally unhappy fate: "More than anything it is the sorrowful fate of Liza, poor Liza, that draws me to the walls of the Se-nov Monastery. Ach! I love those subjects that touch my heart and make me shed tears of tender grief!" Karamzin thus moves his reader's emotions in a straight line toward a set of melancholy expectations concerning the story he is about to tell.

The tale ends as it begins, with the narrator ruminating on the lugubrious impression the locale creates on him. Now, instead of the monastery reverberating with the "groan of time," it is Liza's deserted cottage that is described and, in it, the spirit of poor Liza is groaning. As

Karamzin created a euphonic background for the monastery and its hopeless prisoners, so does he orchestrate his description of the sorrowful cottage and its ghost with an accumulation of back vowels and suggestive sibilants:

> Xižina opustela. V nej voet veter, i suevernye poseljane, slyša po nočam sej šum, govorjat: 'Tam stonet mertvec; tam stonet bednaja Liza'.

> [The cottage became deserted. The wind howls in it and superstitious peasants, hearing this sound in the night, say: 'A corpse groans there; poor Liza groans there!']

Suggestion is more important than explanation when Karamzin adopts the guise of narrator. Delicate associations and reflections emotionally blur the outline of class problems, pain, sex, and death. The narrator's words are richer in musical value than in clarity of conceptualization. The reader's sense of floating in and out of this emotional focus harmonizes with the movement of melodic clauses. As the famous Soviet literary theoretician Eikhenbaum suggests, words are chosen more for their sound value than for their specificity of thought.[6] The sentence, as a suggestive unit of rhythm, is more important than the referential value of any word.[7] At such emotional peaks in the story, nothing is allowed to jar the fragile mood. So, vulgar speech, technical jargon, complex thoughts and mind-taxing clauses are systematically excluded. The result is a train of evocative hints and a hypnotically rhythmical sentence structure that creates what Gukovsky calls a musical rather than an information apprehension of external reality.[8]

The often-heard charge that Karamzin is too restrictive in his choice of words and phrases, and thereby excludes the innate expressiveness of oral Russian [9] is quite correct, at least in those passages presided over by the narrator. in defense of Karamzin, however, it should be pointed out that his narrator's monotonously graceful speech is perfectly adapted to Karamzin's goal of evoking moods of introverted contemplation. Just as his themes avoid contact with problems of society and institutional reform, so does his narrator's language, founded on the new *izjaščnyj vkus* ["refined taste"], avoid any hint of practical engagement with "reality." The "real" world is to be screened out linguistically as it is thematically. In its place there is substituted an ineffable mood; specifics of palpable social problems are purposely subordinated to a welter of emotional connotations.

The emotionally-involved narrator concentrates his reader's attention on feelings of disappointed hope in achieving happiness on this earth. His lyrical descriptions of nature, as well as his feelings about events in the story, consistently accentuate a mood of vague apprehension or open sorrow. Taken together, his role fulfills the sentimental attempt to turn inward, to cultivate a state of mind and heart conducive to contemplating life's unreliability. He consistently disengages the reader from the outside world with its social institutions, logic, and conventional processes of problem solving. He leads his "friend" the reader into a series of experiences that, by his own acknowledgment, reinforce an aura of disappointment and failure. Liza dies, Erast is racked by guilt for life, Liza's mother soon dies. The "groan of time" dominates and the reader, like the narrator, finds himself meditating on the mutability of this life.

The narrator's personality in "Poor Liza" is a constant factor in the story and it is his lyrical responsiveness that determines the pervasive emotional atmosphere of the work. But the narrator is not the only source of commentary in this tale. Karamzin also breaks into the narrative *qua* author to converse directly with the reader about the story's events. In this guise, Karamzin assumes a judgmental, more intellectual voice. As author he rises above the tale's events and characters as well as the emotional personality of the narrator. As the contemporary Soviet literary historian E. N. Kupreyanova points out, Karamzin integrates certain didactic moral principles into the tale as well as creating engaging characters. [10] As commenting author, Karamzin periodically establishes an important distance, both from the touching events of the tale, and from the narrator's emotional amplification of them. As intruding author Karamzin breaks into the narrator's reveries to stand above them and determine what lessons can be learned from those sad events. His use of the auctorial prerogative follows the eighteenth-century didactic tradition with its direct admonitions to the reader. The device was important in the *Letters* and continues to play an analogous role in Karamzin's short fiction. Whereas as narrator he generates a sense of helpless melancholy about the human condition, as philosophizing author he draws clear moral standards against which character behavior is explicitly judged. By introducing principles of moral justice into the work, Karamzin provides an element of stability amidst the emotional foundering of characters and, to some extent, the narrator as well.

Sipovsky considers the author's direct involvement with interpreting his work's moral lessons to be a pronounced fact in most Russian prose of the late eighteenth century and he dates the convention as far back as F. Émin's *Letters of Ernest and Doravra [Pis'ma Ernesta i Doravry]* (1766). [11] The Soviet critic Ju. D. Levin, in his recent discussion of the late eighteenth-century Russian short story, discerns a similar moral directive in it which he traces back to the didactic essays of British journals (especially Addison and Steele's *The Spectator*). [12] Karamzin's use of that exhortation provides a semblance of control in this story and admits a ray of optimism at the end. The author's digressive judgments derive from sentimental doctrine as do the narrator's moments of despair and, together, they provide a miniature cosmos replete with the problems and solutions considered by the philosophy of sensibility.

Authorial digressions arise from the events of the tale but, as is typical of the device historically, they ultimately go beyond those events and aspire to a larger significance. For example, after Erast succeeds in his physical passion for Liza, the author interrupts the narrative with the following moralistic comment:

> He who knows his own heart, who has duly considered the character of its most tender pleasures, he will, of course, agree with me that the fulfillment of *all* desires is the most dangerous temptation of love.

The narrator is an emotional creature who lyrically responds to the events he describes. He is temperamentally incapable of drawing moral lessons from a character's plight. That function is reserved for Karamzin's authorial intrusions in which he exhibits analytical powers, in which he conceptualizes. There are several examples of the intruding author's judgmental commentary. Given the information that Erast is drawing dangerously close to Liza during their secret meetings, the author interjects the advice:

> Rash young man! Do you know your own heart? Can you always be responsible for its urgings? Is good sense always the ruler of your feelings?

Karamzin's didactic presence also applies to his judgments about the characters' background and personality formation. For example, he authorially interrupts the narrative to render the following definition of Erast:

> Now the reader must know that this young man, this Erast, is a rather rich landowner with a rather good mind and a kind heart — kind by nature but weak and inconstant.

There then follows a rather extensive explanation of Erast that corroborates authorial opinion of his weaknesses and penchant for illusion. In his auctorial guise, Karamzin rises to the level of irony in the tale, a device he uses to accentuate the weight of authorial opinion:

> He [Erast] read novels, idylls, had a rather lively imagination and often removed himself in his thoughts back in those times (actual or fictional) in which, if we can believe the poets, every one strolled the fields without a care, bathed in pure springs, kissed like turtle doves, relaxed under roses and myrtle and spent all their days in happy leisure.

Remarks by Karamzin such as those above proceed directly from a reasoning, at times ironical mind in which lyrical transports have no place. As is the case in other tales in this first cycle, authorial opinion (at times manifest in his wit and humor) plays an important role in providing a vantage point from which Karamzin guides the reader toward the proper understanding of what the story is supposed to mean. The intrusions are well marked in the text and function as digressions to the narrative itself. With his above analytical judgment of Erast completed, for example, Karamzin resumes the story proper with the transition: "Let us return to Liza."

"Poor Liza" is an exercise in the sentimental search for alternate forms of reality in which imagination and the power of feeling might be self justifying. The lyrical narrator is Karamzin's main vehicle for leaving the "real" world and entering the realm of introspective sensibility. But the narrator feels more than he can understand and there is a danger that emotion by itself might swamp the reader (along with the narrator) in a sea of relativism (as developed romanticism was prone to do later in the nineteenth century). In sentimentalism, strength of feeling was not the only criterion of the sought-for alternative existence. For Karamzin, as for Rousseau, Marivaux, Richardson, and Sterne, the concept of personal morality was an indispensible requisite. Through his use of the intruding author, Karamzin establishes firm standards of moral justice to which the tale's characters are subject. The reader is told quite clearly by the gnomic author when Erast lives up to those standards and when he fails them. Karamzin's application of those standards to his characters is a central fact of the work's narrative scheme. Both the subjective mood of the tale and its moralistic lessons are central to sentimentalism as a movement. By coordinating them in "Poor Liza" through his manipulation of narrative perspectives Karamzin succeeds in artfully impressing them upon his readers.

"NATALIA THE BOYAR'S DAUGHTER"

"Natal 'ja bojarskaja doc' " ["Natalia the Boyar's Daughter"] (1791) treats a lighter, happier situation than does "Poor Liza." It is the fabricated tale of a mythical author who purports to have heard it from an ancient relative as his mind wandered "in the kingdom of imagination." The plot is concerned with Natalia, the daughter of a famous boyar who lived in ancient Russia. Approaching her eighteenth year Natalia, "like the birds of the forest who nest in pairs," is ready for love. She is strongly attracted to a mysterious young man whom she sees one day in church. He shares her ardor and, after an interview arranged by Natalia's old nurse, the heroine and the young man (Aleksei) elope. Aleksei dares not ask permission of Natalia's father because, as is explained later, Aleksei's father was accused (wrongly) of treason several years earlier and was forced to flee the country. Aleksei had returned to Russia secretly after his father's death in the hope of restoring his family's good name. It was on one of his secret visits to Moscow that he had first seen and fallen in love with Natalia. The young couple lives happily deep in the forest, their only concerns being Aleksei's constant wish to clear his name through some service to the Tsar and Natalia's unhappiness at leaving her grieving father without permission. A war with Lithuania solves both their problems in a *deus ex machina.* Husband and wife go to battle together and, at the decisive moment, rally the troops securing victory for Moscow. As he is thanked personally by the Tsar, Aleksei reveals his name. The Tsar, who already knew of his father's unjust conviction, sheds tears of joy at having Aleksei back home. In the same scene Natalia reveals herself to her father who tearfully welcomes her return. As the story closes, all problems are solved, all characters are happy, and harmony reigns for everyone.

In searching for the beginnings of modern Russian historical prose, attention has at times rested on "Natalia." The setting is old Moscow and different social classes are visible from the Tsar (unnamed) to members of the boyars, down to representatives of the peasant class (Natalia's nurse) and even beggars. Karamzin introduces representative scenes of domestic life in the well-to-do home of Natalia's father in which Karamzin depicts his heroine sewing and braiding lace, spinning silk, or stringing necklaces. Stories about Prince Valadimir alternate with games of blind man's bluff and song-singing to entertain Natalia and her girl friends on long winter evenings. The restrictions of women in Russian society of the day are made visible by the author who says "In the distant past there were no clubs or masquerades where we now go to show ourselves and see others; and so where else, if not in church, could a curious girl go to have a good look at people?" [13] Her father invites the poor to a ritual feast as customs of the time supposedly dictated. Age-old border problems with Lithuania make their way into part of the story, thereby adding a political dimension to the more personal and social details that appear in the tale.

Despite the allusions to cultural values, physical details and vague references to military campaigns, the historical side of the tale is stylized. Karamzin's presentation of social stratification reveals no separate class interests. The poorest beggar and the most influential of boyars are equally content with their lot. The charming old nurse who accompanies Natalia in her adventures is humorous and helps the lovers conspire but she provides no insight into peasant attitudes and class values. Her language, for example, is not differentiated from that of her mistress. The war with Lithuania provides no actual data on Russia's relations with the outside world, nor does Karamzin try to establish any.

The tale cannot adequately serve as the first Russian historical story because issues and detail of the time primarily serve a conventionally sentimental plot and character production. Natalia's father is a model of the upright parent whose love for his child stays constant despite prejudicial evidence. His image does not contain the specifics of his class pursuits. The Tsar is more interested in savoring the touching reunion between father and daughter than he is with his war against Lithuania. The monarch's ability to weep outweighs any practical matters of state. Similarly, Natalia and Aleksei are modern sentimental lovers suited up in ancient dress. Their sensibilities are refined and their love is playfully idealized on the order of Daphnis and Chloe: "Like two robins in the spring that love one another and embrace with their little wings, so did Natalia and Aleksei love each other."

"Natalia" is an idyll played out against Karamzin's version of Russia's Golden Age, "when Russians were Russians, when they dressed in their own clothes, walked with their natural gait, lived according to their own fashion, spoke in their own language . . . " The facade of historical verisimilitude is reflective of the Western tendency in Karamzin's day to paint an idealized picture of moral simplicity in a past, better age with hopes of encouraging the modern reader's emulation in his own complex society. As the fictitious author points out, the idea is "only to impart a light historical touch to the work."

The question of authorial intrusion is of central

importance in "Natalia" for it is that narrative focus which Karamzin chooses to mold his reader's relation to the work's characters and their meaning. The initial impression of the fictional author is that he is a humorous presence who shams the conventional pastoral characters of the story. In his introduction he describes the source of his story as the ghost of his "grandfather's grandmother." He gets along well with her, praising her old fashioned mode of dress over "the contemporary *bonnets à la . . .* and all the Franco-Albion apparel that shines on the Moscow beauties of the late eighteenth century." Nevertheless, he fears making a mess of his tale lest "the old woman set upon me on a cloud from the world beyond and punish me with her crutch for poor eloquence . . . Ach, no! Forgive my foolhardiness, noble shade — you would not do such a thing!"

The playful author has a good deal more to him than waggish chatter, however. Through his overt manipulation of his characters, the description process, and his readers, Karamzin, as intruding author, turns his tale into a running commentary on subjects of his own choosing. The fact that in so doing he exists outside time, relating back to the events he describes, and forward to the contemporary reader, allows him undisturbed freedom in subordinating the tale and its audience to that commentary.

The events that constitute the tale are not original, nor can they be taken seriously in themselves. The light tone Karamzin fosters, together with the artificially saccharine ending of the story, insulates the reader from the kind of emotional involvement that characterizes "Poor Liza." The fabula does not form the center of attention in the work and the intruding author often plays with it in the reader's presence. The historical context and the tale's characters function more as a convenient backdrop against which Karamzin projects a series of digressions. These digressions outweigh the events that suggest them. They free the author to set aside his historical facade, along with his characters, and expand on various sentimental ideals in direct discourse with the reader. Some digressions are seriously phrased while others are colored by broad humor. However, both forms share a unified didactic purpose.

Authorial digressions, with their condensed positing of one or another sentimental value, appear regularly through Karamzin's story, forming didactic peaks. An example of one such peak illustrates its nature. In his description of Natalia and Aleksei's marital bliss, Karamzin uses a small misunderstanding between them to point up their underlying devotion to one another. With their difference quickly resolved, they are pictured as even more happy than before. Karamzin auctorially breaks into the narrative saying:

> Now I should describe the happiness of the young married lovers, hidden by the forest's shadow from the whole world; but you, who delight in the same happiness, tell me, is it possible to describe it? . . . Ach! the pleasures of love are always the same yet always new and without number.

With the author acting as intermediary, the sentimental principle of romantic love is generalized beyond the scene in which it appears; it becomes equally relevant to the past of the story and to the present of the reader. The aphorism that concludes the digression (i.e., "the pleasures of love are always the same yet always new and without number") tightens the message of the whole digression into a striking phrase the reader can easily carry with him as he is returned to the tale's developing plot.

On the same question of romantic love and its irrational power over man, Karamzin describes Natalia's passion for Aleksei. Under its promptings she agrees to marry him and leave her father's house without his knowledge. The author interrupts the narration with the following digression:

> Together with the reader we sincerely blame Natalia, sincerely reproach her for, only having seen the young man three times and having heard a few pleasant words from him, she has decided to run away from her parental home with him, knowing not where. To hand over one's fate to an unknown man whom one could well consider suspicious by his own words and, what is more, to leave a kind, tender, dear father . . . But such is terrible love! It can make a criminal of the most virtuous person! And whoever has passionately loved in his life, but never behaved counter to strict morality, that person is fortunate! He is fortunate because his passion was not at odds with virtue, — otherwise he would admit its weakness and the tears of futile repentance would flow like a river. The chronicles of the human heart assure us of this sad truth.

The competing forces of passionate love and the sanctity of the family, the horns of many a sentimental dilemma, figure prominently in this digression. As in the first example above, the events of the tale expand under the author's hand to a wider significance. Example leads to generalization, the past gains momentum as it reinforces sentimental considerations of the present.

The competing attractions of love between parent and child on the one hand, and romantic love on the other, characterize a number of authorial intrusions. The fact that Natalia's father adores her is pointedly elevated to a general principle the author impresses upon us: "Reader! Do you know by actual experience the feelings of a parent?" The author then proceeds into a long aside to explain the power of that affection. Commiserating with the father at Natalia's disappearance, the author expounds on the cruelty of fate, even in the face of the purest of parental virtues: "Henceforth, good boyar, your life will be enshrouded by the shadow of grief." As in other digressions, the intruding author is given to finish his remarks with an aphorism: "Alas! Virtue itself cannot save us from sorrow!"

Romantic love exerts an opposing pressure in the tale which receives a good deal of the author's commentary. The application of its power also extends beyond the characters, applying to the reader's context as well. When Natalia senses the stirrings of physical love in herself the author addresses the reader with the rhetorical question: "Ach! Why does the most tender, the most fiery of the passions appear alongside sadness; for what lover does not sigh, what lover does not despair during the first days of his passion, thinking his beloved does not return his love?" In other places he pauses to point out that a lover's passion is never satisfied and a lover is like a miser in that they both cannot get their fill of admiring and loving the object of their affection. In each case, the intruding author carefully draws his reader into the digression through rhetorical address or generalization.

Particularly interesting are those numerous digressions in which the author combines his gnomic tendencies with comic elements. These are especially intriguing in their formal aspects because, as with earlier practitioners of the comic in sentimental fiction, Karamzin's editorial humor serves a serious purpose. For example, there is a scene in which Natalia first experiences the nameless agitations of mature love. Disturbed by her mistress's obvious discomfort, the nurse is sure that someone has put a spell on her charge and she tries to ward it off with "pious remarks" and signs of the cross. The author strictly controls the emotional potential of the scene with the following comic digression:

> Ach, good crone! Although you lived on this earth a good while, there was still a good deal you did not know. You did not know why or what begins to happen in girls of boyar families at a certain age; you did not know ... But, perhaps the reader also (if they still hold this book in their hands and are not dozing off), — perhaps the readers also do not know what a misfortune suddenly happened to our heroine, what her eyes sought in her chamber, why she sighed, cried, grieved. It is well known that up to now she was as happy as a free little bird, that her life flowed like a clear stream over little white stones between verdant flowering banks; what happened to her? Modest muse, explain! ... − − − From the heavenly azure firmament, and perhaps from somewhere higher, there flew down, like a little humming bird that fluttered, fluttered on the pure spring air and flew into Natalia's tender heart — *the need to love, to love, to love!!!* Here is the whole riddle;

> here is the reason for the beautiful girl's sadness
> — and if it seems not quite understandable to
> any of my readers, then just let him demand the
> most detailed explanation from the eighteen-
> year-old girl who is beloved by him.

Behind his playful, almost satirical handling of the scene, Karamzin develops a serious didactic strategem. Fixing humorous limitations on his thematic context, he isolates and develops the question of romantic love in general terms that include the contemporary reader. Barriers of historical distance are leaped and the explicit concept of love's force emerges clearly for general consideration. With the event that leads up to the principle kept under intellectual control by the author's verbal humor, he is free to move from example to principle, from past to present, without becoming bogged down in the specifics of the scene. In short, the author exercises his Olympian powers to make both his characters and his readers relate equally to the issue of his choice. The constant factor in his verbal games remains his overt emphasis on the concept of love's force.

Karamzin repeats his rhetorical-humorous manipulation of character, event and reader in a number of places. After wittily explaining that Natalia did not read Locke or Rousseau because, first they were not yet alive and, second, because she was illiterate, he expounds on the values of the natural life and how nature instructs simple people in everything they need to know (a paraphrase of Rousseau's popular dictum). Even as he apologizes for his digression, avowedly like those of Sterne, he compounds it with an additional discussion on the uncontrollable demands that love makes on women. They cannot be content with childhood's satisfactions behond a certain age: "No, girls, no! Your heart wishes for something else: it pines for a heart that beats violently whenever it comes close." Forestalling the reader's incredulity at his having the heroine fall desperately in love with the hero only having seen him once, the author wags his finger at us: "In one minute? — the reader will ask. — Having seen him for the first time and not hearing a word from him? Dear sirs! I am relating exactly what happened." With the reader's attention successfully diverted from his plot through the ploy of humor, the author proceeds directly into a ringing address on the power of love:

> Do not doubt the truth; do not doubt the strength of the mutual attraction which two hearts feel when they are made for one another! And whoever does not believe in that concord, go away and do not read our story which is meant only for those tender hearts who have a sweet faith!

Of course, the entire introduction in which the author explains how he heard the story of Natalia is a comic romp with the reader. The image of his "grandfather's grandmother" alternatingly telling him the tale and chasing him with her crutch, prepares us for something other than emotional involvement in the story's events. Karamzin was translating part of *Tristram Shandy* while writing "Natalia" and he was very enthusiastic about the "Story of Le Fever" from Sterne's book. The great English novelist's use of the comic digression is clear in this tale. The union of comic and serious elements in the figure of an intruding author is not limited to Sterne, however. Wayne Booth traces it back to both Sterne and Fielding (in *Joseph Andrews*) and, ultimately, to *Don Quixote*. [14] All these predecessors, like their Russian student, indulge in romantic irony through which they temporarily suspend the illusion of their work. The retardation of described events shifts reader attention to the author himself. As Henri Fluchére, a contemporary Western critic of Sterne's prose, points out in his discussion of *Tristram Shandy*, those retardations have their roots sunk deep in the history of didactic literature. [15] In Booth's analysis of the comic digression, discerning its nugget of serious instruction, one finds as much relevance to Karamzin as to Fielding, whom Booth is discussing:

> As a rhetorician, an author finds that some of the beliefs on which a full appreciation of his work depends come ready-made, fully accepted by the postulated reader as he comes to the book, and some must be implanted and reinforced . . . . Yet there is a surprising amount of commentary directed to reinforcing values which most readers, one would think, already take for granted. [16]

In Sterne's case, critics were not always so understanding of the gnomic digressions. [17]

One should not be surprised or led astray by Karamzin's mixture of "serious" digressions with those of a "comic" nature any more than earlier readers were by Sterne's use of those elements. For both authors, the mental agility that underpins the ironic digression is just as legitimate a means for raising the reader's vision to some important sentimental ideal as is a straight-forward plea for its consideration. John Traugott, a recent American commentator on Sterne's prose, uses the comparison of a clown in describing the English novelist's sober purpose behind the comic digression. Sterne, says Traugott, urges that "his theory of instruction through wit . . . should be considered as seriously as any clown's efforts to communicate." [18] Karamzin understood Sterne's varied use of digressions better than his Russian contemporaries. [19] He, like the English master, plays with concepts of time and the digression to draw both "historical" character and contemporary reader into a primary relationship with specific sentimental principles. Those principles transcend both time contexts as the intruding author wanders at will between past and present, espousing issues, along with their applicability, within whichever time frame he chooses.

Before Sterne, time was approached as an objective and mechanical reality which moved linearly through a piece of fiction. "Time was neither the novelist's friend nor his enemy. It was a piece of impersonal data, like the different parts of the plot considered objectively. The writer proceeded from one point to another in a straight line in a given direction at a chosen pace . . ." [20] Sterne was historically responsible for overcoming the limits of linear time progression in the novel. The chief device for that disruption is, again, the digression. The author's self-conscious shift back and forth in time functions to place his digressive remarks above the events he describes. It also reinforces his dominion over the reader's relation to event and character as discussed above, allowing the author periodically to point our attention to didactic peaks in the work.

The time shift as an element of the authorial control also speeds the plot along for Karamzin, much as it did for Fielding and Sterne. The author's self-proclaimed power to artificially break into the plot keeps his presence clearly before the reader. Aleksei sends a runner to determine how

Natalia's father is taking her elopement. The author intrudes saying: "But we shall anticipate what this messenger will learn and take a look at what is happening in the imperial city [Moscow] ." Later, Karamzin drops his description of Aleksei and Natalia's exploits in battle to switch back to the city again: "But let us leave our young couple for a short time, in the hope that heaven will not abandon them . . . Let us return to Moscow — there our story began, there it must end."

At times, the author exerts his control over time and the reader's expectations to play a trick on the unwary reader. As Natalia arrives at Aleksei's forest retreat and sees its armed inhabitants, her nurse is sure they have fallen into the hands of robbers. The author then intrudes saying "Now I could present a terrible picture for the readers' eyes." He could, he asserts, tell a tale of Natalia's plight in the hands of the cruel and terrible barbarians, forced to witness vicious scenes of pillage and mayhem. Moving his fanciful narrative ahead in time, he says he could portray Natalia's future capture and execution before the horrified eyes of her father. After purposely manipulating the reader's contemplation of a whole series of sad events that would "make a sensitive person shed tears of sorrow and grief," the author explodes his fabrication with a flourish explaining "No, dear reader, no! Save your tears this time — calm down — the old nurse was mistaken."

The result of the farcical narrative insert, so reminiscent of Sterne's Le Fever and, later, Gogol's Captain Kopeikin, is a reinforced image of the author as absolute master of all that occurs in the story. He leads us down the garden path as an audacious exhibition of his powers; we are totally reliant on him for events and their interpretation. Therefore, when he tells his reader to believe in one or another sentimental principle, as he does in many digressions, the reader has no choice but to rely on his discursive opinion. He is his own center of judgment in the story.

Karamzin's mingling of his "historical" tale's fabula with modern principles of sentimental taste extends also to questions of his language manipulation. Throughout his tale he integrates vivid Russian folk expressions and archaic words into a rich matrix of Western-inspired phrases common to sentimental usage of his own time. The Western cliches are generally based on calques and characteristically incorporate periphrasis (one of the favorite stylistic devices of the sentimental movement). Such contemporary terms as *cvety ljubvi* ["flowers of love"], *predmet ljubvi* ["subject of love"], *predmet nežnyx pobuždenij* ["subject of tender promptings"], *vesna žizni* ["the Spring of life"], *sladkie slezy nežnosti* ["sweet tears of tenderness"], *trogatel'nyj čelovek* ["a touching person"], mix with such traditional or archaic Russian expressions as *v Moskve belokamennoj* ["in white-stoned Moscow"], *velikij xlebosol* ["a notable host"], *krasnye devuški* ["beautiful girls"], *zlatoglavaja Moskva* ["gold-crowned Moscow"], *dobryj bojarin* ["the good boyar"], *bradatyj* ["bearded"], *solncy* ["suns"], *čeloveki* ["men"], or the traditional negative definition of folk poetry, *on byl neobidčikom a pokrovitelem* ["he was not one to insult, but a protector"].

In his discussion of that stylistic mixture, A. I. Efimov, a contemporary Soviet critic of style, points out that the striking Russian expressions are much in the minority compared to Karamzin's accumulation of sentimental phraseology. He concludes that the mingling is in keeping with Karamzin's goal of adding only a dash of Russian flavor to a fundamentally Western mode of expression. [21] The juxtaposition of the two phraseological systems is often close syntactically. The Western-inspired expression *"magazin piitičeskix upodoblenij"* ["the store-house of poetic comparisons"] occurs in the same paragraph as the old Russian expression *"znat' gramote"* ["to be literate"]. *"Zlatoglavaja Moskva"* ["Gold-crowned Moscow"] is in the same paragraph as the traditional Western personification *"prelestnaja skromnost'"* ["charming modesty"]. *"Vsjakaja vsjačina"* ["This and that"] occurs within a few lines of the invoked Greek nymph of the woods, the dryad. The ironic or humorous incongruity of Karamzin's mixture of archaic or folk Russian phrases with contemporary Western expressions fits the intruding author's penchant for the same narrative tone. It also reiterates Karamzin's overall manipulation of the fabula to frame event and character in terms of contemporary sentimental taste. [22]

"Natalia" is a very different tale from "Poor Liza" even though they were written within a few months of one another. The emotionally vibrant narrator who virtually transfixed the reader by his sympathetic involvement with Liza and Erast is all but gone in "Natalia." Here the narrator, as a limited and emotional presence, is anachronistic, appearing briefly, almost as an afterthought in the epilog. He wanders along the banks of the Moscow River and finds Aleksei and Natalia's grave stone which he reads "with the greatest difficulty." The attempt at veracity carries as little weight in this story as it was effective in "Poor Liza." The reduction of the structured narrator in "Natalia" is consistent, however, with Karamzin's experimentation with the use of authorial humor. Any sustained emotional pitch in the tale would compromise Karamzin's system of didactic digressions, based as it often is on comic principles.

"THE BEAUTIFUL PRINCESS
AND THE FORTUNATE DWARF"

Karamzin's other treatment of pseudo-history appears in "Prekrasnaja carevna i ščastlivyj karla" ["The Beautiful Princess and the Fortunate Dwarf"] (1792) which he wrote within a few months of "Natalia." Although he terms the piece a fairy tale *(starinnaja skazka)*, it shares major thematic and narrative schemata with its immediate predecessor. Also, like "Natalia," this story didactically spreads prime beliefs of sentimentalism in a comic context. "The Beautiful Princess" is a whimsical treatment of the Prince-and-the-Frog theme. The story proper begins with the Russian fairy tale cliché *"V nekotorom carstve, v nekotorom gosudarstve žil-byl Car' dobryj čelovek."* ["In a certain kingdom, in a certain country there once lived Tsar Good Man."] [23] (the Russian equivalent of the Western formula "Once upon a time in a faraway kingdom there lived a good king.")

A simplified anecdote, the tale takes as its subject a beautiful princess who is besieged by innumerable suitors from as many kingdoms. When the king, her father, urges her to choose one as her husband she refuses them all, preferring the solitude of her tower to marriage. The king sadly sends the suitors away and resigns himself to reigning over his land without the prospect of an heir. A wizard who happens by rewards the king's hospitality with a clue to the problem of the princess's refusal. She is in love but wishes to hide the name of her choice. Confronting his daughter with her secret, the knowledge of which he explains as having come to him in a dream, the king demands an explanation. The princess still refuses to answer. The enigma is soon solved when the king happens upon his daughter in the embrace of her lover, the court dwarf. The shocked king cannot verbalize his surprise and retires. Karamzin then interrupts the story to explain the reasons for the dwarf's attractiveness to the princess. Realizing that he would never be of normal size or handsome in appearance, the dwarf had concentrated on developing his spiritual faculties — a powerful voice, a profound mind, refined artistic talents, and a commitment to the wisdom of moral ideals. Without knowing it, the dwarf had won the princess' love through those inner qualities of the spirit (Karamzin's version of the kiss bestowed by the princess on the charmed prince). After some hesitation he returned her love. The king, once he determines the purity of the lovers' mutual attachment, willingly gives his consent to the marriage. Announcing their betrothal to his assembled subjects, the king reminds them of the dwarf's past services in halting an invading army of giants by playing his reed pipes before their fierce king. To the resounding cheers of the crowd, the marriage is performed on the spot. In predictable fairy tale fashion, the son-in-law eventually succeeds to the throne when the king dies. He is a good ruler and lives happily ever after with the princess.

Karamzin's "new" version of the fairy tale is, of course, hardly serious on its surface. It is no more distinctively Russian in its character definitions or in the recounting of their adventures than was his "historical" tale of a year earlier. The kingdom is unnamed (it seems a mixture of Old Russia and a Western fairy tale castle); none of the characters are given names. In this respect, Karamzin was representative of his age which was prone to mix romance clichés of knightly gallantry with weak national folk elements. [24] The magician who visits the Tsar is dressed "in a tall cap on which the moon and stars [are] represented," more reminiscent of Merlin than anything Russian. The suitors are alternately called "princes" and *carevici;* they sing under the heroine's window in couplets like troubadours. The dwarf himself is incongruously (for a Russian folk tale) described as a new Demosthenes who perfects his rhetorical powers by reciting his own verbal compositions to the ocean's waves.

"The Beautiful Princess" does, however, like "Natalia," have an instructive dimension to its whimsy. There is present here the same relationship between a light veil of distant time and place and viable issues of modern sentimentalism as appeared in "Natalia." By way of putting new wine into old bottles Karamzin reworks certain elements of the eighteenth-century adventure romance in this tale to enhance the visibility of newer sentimental attitudes (i.e., the superiority of spiritual purity over physical attractiveness, the success of Platonic love despite social barriers of class and station, and an idealized sense of devotion between parent and child). For example, the wizard's prophecy, the Tsar's dream in which fiery words are magically written in a cave in answer to his questions about the future, a father's objections to his daughter's choice of suitors, and the hero's single-handed victory over great odds, all represent favorite ingredients of the old-fashioned adventure romance. [25] But, Karamzin alters each of these external impediments to his lovers to sketch in schematic form the idea of internal, psychological conflicts in his characters. In this reworking of romance, Karamzin followed the lead of the "new novel" of sentimentalism, greatly simplifying it in the process. [26] For example, the Tsar's desire to have his daughter marry and present an heir to the throne is in conflict with his desire to see her happy. The dwarf at first refuses to return the princess' love because of the class differences separating them (he is lowborn) as well as his physical deformity. The princess is in a quandary as to whether to disclose to her father her love for the dwarf or keep her secret, thereby saving the king from the shock of learning her lover's identity.

There is no question of those sentimental, psychological issues finding a serious platform there. As he did in "Natalia," Karamzin schematizes their complications to fit a didactic plan. The tale's value is that of a light sketch of key sentimental values and its appeal is to the reader's wit rather than to his feelings.

Karamzin maintains his jocose postulation of sentimental issues by his verbal play much as he did in "Natalia." Again he mixes sentimental phraseology with archaic Russian forms, and in the same measure. The folk simile comparing the princess to a swan *(kak gordyj lebed')* appears in the same line as the modern periphrasis *zvezda ljubvi* ["the star of love"], also used to describe the princess. The folk topos *skazyvat' skazki* ["to tell tales"] appears in the same sentence with the sentimental phrases *svjatye dobrodeteli* ["sacred virtues"] and the periphrasis *dolina žizni* ["the vale of life"]. Within a few lines of one another there appears the modern calque *krylataja boginja nazyvaemaja Slava* ["the winged goddess called Glory"] which is juxtaposed to the folk formula *iz-za tridevjati zemel* ["from far far away"]. The Russian folk cliché *stol dubovyj* ["oaken tale"] contrasts sharply with the *umil'nye glaza* ["touching eyes"] of the suitors. Verging on open laughter he presents the folk princess "casting her blue eyes to the ground" *[potupla v zemlju golubye glaza svoi]* only to indulge in the mock-serious description of her "two gleaming tears" which roll down her cheeks like two droplets of rain which are wafted away from a rose by the breath of a zephyr."

The personalized narrator is hardly present in Karamzin's tale as was the case in "Natalia." He appears only in his superficial capacity of lending the barest fabrication of verisimilitude. He appears early in the tale to assure the reader that the physical description of the princess he is about to introduce is reliable: "In an ancient archive I happened to stumble across one of these descriptions — here is its faithful translation." Then, at the end of the tale, he again appears to convey history's high opinion of the dwarf's good deeds while king. The narrator hardly qualifies as an introspective personality; he is devoid of the emotional appeal of his predecessor in "Poor Liza."

The explanation for the narrator's lack of emotional involvement or interpretive role in this work lies in the use Karamzin makes of its characters and events. His exclusion of all specificity of detail, all lyrical description, and any play of subtle associations in the narrator, fit his use of the tale as an anecdote. The fact that the narrator does not relate to the characters emotionally helps maintain their simplicity and geometrical clarity. Karamzin leads the reader to expect a pasteboard treatment of character by his subtitle for the story *Starinnaja skazka ili novaja karikatura* ["An Ancient Fairy Tale or a New Caricature"].

The narrative process here, as in "Natalia," is organized around the intruding author and his penchant for humor and digressions. He playfully manipulates the tale's superficial fabula to isolate and make visible to the reader selected sentimental situations and themes. Assuming the voice of editorial authority, Karamzin weaves gnomic commentaries into the comic fabric of the tale. He periodically punctuates the story with directives as to how to interpret its ultimate meaning, and what lessons the reader is to draw from it. He asserts his instructive prerogative before the story proper begins, laying before us the central sentimental principle of the work (i.e., the superiority of spiritual beauty over physical attributes as a basis for love):

> O you uncomely sons of mankind, deformed creations of capricious Nature! You who can in no way serve as a model to the artist when he wants to represent the elegance of the human form! You who complain against Nature and say that it has not given you the means to please, that it has blocked for you the source of life's sweetest pleasure — the source of love! Do not despair, my friends, and believe that you can still be appealing and loved; that today or tomorrow the obliging zephyrs can bring you a charming Psyche who will throw herself into your embraces with delight and who will say there is nothing dearer than you on earth. Listen to the following tale to its end.

Sensibility's *sine qua non* that meaningful relationships in life spring from the beauty of one's soul rather than from one's external appearance or social position conceptually rings through this invocation. The extended rhetorical address, the balanced clause structure with repeated key words, emphasize Karamzin's editorial directive. His accentuation of negative forms in the first half (relating to physical attributes) is balanced by an answering series of positive remarks about hope in life stemming from individual spiritual qualities. All elements thus combine forcefully to press upon the reader the intruding author's intended lesson.

 Correlative to the issue of spiritual superiority are

authorial pronouncements concerning the general moral superiority of the Golden Age to modern times. In the past, says the intruding author, "poets were not such flatterers as they are now; they did not call black white, a dwarf a giant, and ugliness an example of gracefulness." The assumption is that such distorted values typify modern society. Questions of love were more poignant in the past because of people's sensitivity. The author assures us that the delicacy of feeling has been lost in the more jaded present:

> You should know that lovers in the distant past were as shy and retiring as pretty maidens, and they did not dare express their love in words to the masters of their hearts. In our times they are much bolder but as a consequence *eloquence of the gaze* has lost almost all its power.

In the same vein, the commenting author assures his reader that, like lovers and poets, rulers in the past were in tune with true values of moral leadership. The Tsar's usual attitude is one of governing "as a father guides his children, of spreading prosperity in his country — a matter [the author emphasizes] which is sacred and pleasurable!" What would be an *urok carjam* ["a lesson to the king"] in the hands of the philosophers of Enlightenment assumes, for Karamzin's more sentimental commentator-author, the tone of an encomium to the past's natural piety.

The complementary ideals of spiritual rather than physical criteria for love, and the greater morality of the remote past over the present, so familiar in Western sentimental literature, are the prime lessons the commenting author urges here. His faith that the reader can both learn those lessons and act upon them is at the bottom of his didactic task. The lessons show through especially clearly because of the work's facile plot and uni-dimensional characters. Problems that impede the successful fruition of those ideals are solved simply and rapidly. For example, the king discovers the identity of his daughter's lover, discusses the issue with them, calls the populace together for consultation, and marries the couple all within a period of twenty-four hours. Nothing diverts reader attention from the clear lesson of how morality and spiritual purity succeed.

Karamzin further emphasizes the work's moralism by discussing directly with the reader the stories the dwarf tells to the princess. In one sense they are miniature reflections of the larger tale itself. On the surface they are small folk tales about water witches and evil magicians. The point of each, however, like the parent work, directly accentuates simplified moral lessons worthy of popular English sentimental novels. Some of the dwarf's stories stress the happiness that results from retaining a private sense of virtue. Others point out the reverse, the terrible wages of personal sin. The dwarf tells her other stories of virtuous lovers who weather the many "temptations of fate" and are rewarded by "the fullness of earthly bliss." His remarks leave the reader with the distinct impression that capsulized versions of *Pamela* and *Clarissa* have found their way into the distant Russian past.

The specifics of Karamzin's comic use of the intruding author are much akin to those in "Natalia," guaranteeing the reader a sense of emotional removal from the characters and their adventures (hardly a problem in this story). In this sense, the elimination of a viable narrator and the emphasized presence of the author's humorous digressions contribute to the same distancing effect as discussed in "Natalia." In the process, the

personae become even more schematized as mere extensions of prominent sentimental concepts. Comic asides
appear regularly to break up potentially serious moments.
One of the downcast suitors, rejected by the princess, is
described by the intruding author as fixing his gaze on his
nose "like an Indian Brahman." Together, the suitors let
out such a sigh at their failure to win the princess's hand
that "the stone walls of the castle were almost toppled."
In the Sternian spirit of turning a poignant love scene into
a nonsense digression, Karamzin as author breaks into his
description of the dwarf and princess's love declaration. He
spins the extraneous yarn of another unusual love situation
in which an unnamed king falls madly in love with frog's
eyes. For him, they are more valuable than youth, beauty
or knowledge.

As in "Natalia," Karamzin also turns editorial humor
to the task of switching into and out of fabula time. The
effect of that break in plot action exhibits and emphasizes
the commenting author's power over his creation — the
characters and the ordering of its events. The time switch
reinforces his status as ultimate authority in the work and
further makes the reader dependent upon him (together
with his instructive penchant) for its meaning. Given the
necessity of explaining the dwarf's remarkable talents and
services that predate the tale's events, the author breaks
into his narration to move into that earlier time frame. The
chronology switch is executed by the author's use of a
humorous remark that disengages the reader from the plot:
" 'How, how could the beautiful princess fall in love with a
humpbacked dwarf' the reader will ask — or not ask."
Going on with his game, the author sets Shakespeare at
odds with the psychologists as to the reason (or its lack)
for love. He then turns the ruse of his digression to present
the dwarf's personal background. With his biographical

task completed, he moves back into *fabula* time via the comic digression about frogs' eyes mentioned above and the transition phrase "Now let us return to our story." Smoothly picking up where he left off, the author works his way back to where he first broke the original narrative: "We said that *Tsar Good Man* slammed the door and went out of the princess's tower, but did we not say where he went? Well, let the readers know that he went to his own chamber, . . . ''

Because Karamzin treats sentimental issues with humor does not mean that he no longer believes in their value. The validity of love based on spiritual rather than physical or social qualities, or the competition between simultaneous desires in a single person are not denied in these tales because Karamzin views them through the glass of wit. It is important to keep "Natalia" and "The Beautiful Princess" distinct from mockery or farce. Each tale serves to isolate and clarify specific sentimental canons, canons which were necessary for the Russian reader to understand and with which he had yet to gain a thorough familiarity. By exposing his readers to selected sentimental articles of faith via humor and the emotional distance therein implied, Karamzin controlled the complexity of those questions and made them easier to acquire for the Russian initiate into the New Sensibility.

"JULIA"

"Julija" ["Julia"] [27] (1794) was written later than the other stories considered in this chapter and represents yet another genre. It nevertheless maintains the didactic momentum characteristic of those tales and continues to display Karamzin's narrative emphasis common to them. Its major thematic concerns underscore important sentimental ideals; its narrative structure retains an emphasis on the teaching, directive presence of an intruding author. Karamzin uses that mode to again establish links between the particulars of theme and character in the work and the general truths of broader sentimental principles. In some respects "Julia" is experimental in that it contains a multi-sided portrait of the heroine's personality which deserves attention in its own right. Unlike her predecessors in this cycle of tales, Julia is a developed and complex character whose personality and values change with the altered circumstances of her life. She maintains reader interest in addition to her value as an illustration for those ideals of sensibility and morality that Karamzin propagates in the story. The creation of a sustained character within the familiar thematics of didacticism reflects a higher level of sophistication in Karamzin's literary vision. The result is the most esthetically interesting story Karamzin has yet produced.

The tale is set in modern Russia and is concerned with the social adventures of Julia, a rare beauty much sought after by suitors. She initially plays the role of coquette to the applause of Moscow society but, as she approaches her twentieth year, she feels the inclination to marry. She apparently is on the verge of accepting the proposal of Aris, a paragon of virtue: "a knowledge of what is worthy and pleasant crowned his soul, virtuous rules governed his heart . . . and the fire of inner sensibility animated his gaze." What appears to be a perfect match between Julia's beauty and Aris's moral goodness is cut short by Prince N., a social lion who is utterly lacking in any spiritual development. The flighty girl chooses the prince's shallow charm to Aris's depth of virtue. Turning away from Aris, Julia expects the prince's romantic interest to lead to the altar and is hard pressed to keep her chastity. When the prince realizes that love and marriage are inseparable for Julia he abruptly leaves town, coldly explaining by letter that marriage would only spoil his feeling for the heroine. She is crushed but saves her pride by marrying Aris whose steadfast devotion has never wavered.

The couple moves out of Moscow and its pernicious society to enjoy the country with its atmosphere of moral vigor and natural beauty. As Julia says: "only in the rustic quiet, only in the embrace of nature can the sensitive heart fully rejoice in love and tenderness!" The honeymoon is a short one, however, and Julia is soon drawn back to the glitter of that same society she had recently scorned. The faithful Aris takes her back to Moscow with the unhappy consequence that Julia renews her relationship with Prince N. Finding them in a *tête-à-tête*, Aris flees. He communicates to his wife by letter that he is leaving her to her freedom while resigning himself to wander about the world alone.

Julia finally understands her foolishness and returns to their country home alone, forsaking the city and its false ways forever. She learns she is pregnant and, influenced by her reading of Rousseau's *Émile*, devotes her life to the natural education of her and Aris's son. The years go by as Julia's life becomes a harmonious synthesis of sincere penitence, pure love for her absent husband, true dedication to her son's physical and moral growth, and a pervasive sweet melancholy in response to her personal lot of life. Learning that Julia has truly given up her old attachments to pleasure-oriented society (in the Rousseauian spirit which permeates the story), Aris returns to forgive and forget her moral transgressions of the past. The story ends with a full reconciliation and the establishment of complete familial harmony.

"Julia" is a much more complex work than its predecessors. There is a basic tension in it between simplified thematics and complex character production which points to experimentation and growth in Karamzin's prose art. In one sense the tale continues the propagation of arch sentimental *topoi.* In this respect characters serve as living examples of established sentimental attitudes toward society, nature and the family. Karamzin's black-and-white juxtaposition of urban society's moral degradation and the spiritual purity of intimate contact with nature permeates the story thematically. Julia is a walking object lesson about the dangers of the former and the rewards of the latter. At the same time, she transcends her function of a uni-dimensional testimonial to moral values and achieves individual identity vis-à-vis the reader. In this sense, fabula situations provide a variety of stimuli that exhibit growth and change in Julia as an individual and are secondary to that growth.

Approaching "Julia" via the question of its narrative structure is particularly helpful in unraveling Karamzin's closely-knit relationship between theme and character. The didactic tendencies of the story, as with those preceding it, are primarily the responsibility of the intruding author. His opinions and urgings establish the clearest bonds between general sentimental values and the specifics of events and character behavior in the work. Karamzin's auctorial presence is consistent throughout the story, leading the reader into the proper perception of what happens and explaining how to interpret it. As outspoken author he establishes Julia as the most sought-after woman of capital society: "Is it necessary to mention that all the young men adored Julia and considered it an honor to adore her?" Envious female rivals try to find a flaw in her charms but, as the author remarks, "A vain hope!" He keeps in clear view his opinions of the games in which vain society indulges. He mocks its frivolous attitudes toward love, stating:

> Such love is no joke! You will say that in the days of chivalry they loved differently — My dear sirs! Every age has its own customs: we live in the eighteenth century!

He then proceeds to expound his views of chivalry's demise in the present.

Speaking in the voice of the commenting author, superior in his knowledge of the *fabula* he unrolls, Karamzin directs the reader in his expectation of events to come, much as Fielding did in his novels (e.g., "Aris will not deceive Julia; but Julia — we shall see!"). The author's commentary is pervasive and few events transpire without the stamp on his opinion. In a short aside late in the tale he proudly points with approbation to Julia's sensitized moral state in nature: "Is it necessary to mention that it was she who nursed her own son?" He also expands the scope of his opinion to treat the general faults of social priorities, rendering his own sermon in the process. At one point he belabors its misplaced preference for glitter and superficial charm over quiet spiritual depth:

> Does society sense the value of such people [as Aris]? Rarely. There tinsel is preferred at times to real gold; modesty, the friend of merit, remains in shadow while impertinence earns fame and applause.

The main distinction between the intruding author's role in "Julia" and his appearance in earlier tales is that in

"Julia" Karamzin has his characters participate directly in the work's didactic design along with the intruding author. Julia's or Aris's monologs contain resounding attacks on modern urban life and its moral laxity which echo the very opinions Karamzin preaches in editorial omniscience. The characters' vigorous assurances that moral certitude and peace are to be found amidst the wisdom of nature, for example, directly repeat auctorial opinions in the work. The rhetorical value of this arrangement is high as authorial assertion unites with "spontaneous" testimony of the characters themselves. The result is a modern version of the ancient rhetorical principle of variation and restatement of a single opinion. Moreover, the two presentations of any given sentimental value appear very close together in the text. The character's remark often appears first and usually refers to the character's own life experiences. Immediately thereafter, the intruding author draws on the character's remark, expanding it into a general principle. For example, as she returns to the country after having destroyed her marriage, Julia says:

> I am returning alone, a poor widow, but with a heart that loves virtue. It will be my comfort, my friend, my companion, I shall see and kiss its image in the traces of unforgettable Aris!

The digressing author seizes on the heroine's new-found resolve and generalizes on its moral strength once it is clearly understood:

> One has to give you credit, dear women: when you decide on something, not in a moment of flightiness, not by mere words, but with your soul and with a deep feeling of truth; your

firmness then is amazing — and the most glori-
fied Heroes of constancy, whom history praises
to the sky, must share their laurels with you.

In the fervor of her new moral awakening, Julia
dedicates her life to the departed Aris. Her determination
is exemplary, as expressed in her own words:

Your dear shadow is with me; the memory of
your love is with me: I shall not die of grief! I
want to live so that you might have a sympathetic friend on earth.

Immediately after her monolog, the commenting author
digresses to explain the principle which lies beneath her
discovery:

Virtuous feelings cannot co-exist with grief: the
most bitter tears of repentence contain something sweet in them. The dawn of virtue is
beautiful; but then, what else is repentence.

Julia is the chief source of "spontaneous" testimony
on moral ideals. Here is one of her typical denunciations of
conventional values in society:

You [women in society] do not sense the value
of a tender, virtuous heart; you wish to please
the whole world, you chase after brilliant
conquests, and become a sacrifice to your own
vanity.*

The style Karamzin gives Julia's remarks is formal and
declamatory, much like that of the intruding author. She,

like him, resorts to the same use of parallel clauses, each of which begins with the same word. Her stylistic choice of rhetorical address, implying a reference to a whole category of people, expands the application of her thoughts to the level of a principle. Her choice of language and her rhetorical figures are indistinguishable from those the intruding author uses throughout the story. Within the rhetorical design of the work, then, a character assumes a didactic task equal to that of the commenting author himself. Character and author function in unison repeating the same program of values. The asterisk in Julia's speech refers the reader to the author's footnote in which he forcefully supports the heroine's homily:

> 'Is such a conclusion in order' the critic will say:
> 'Can a woman in a situation *of that sort* preach
> virtue?' *She can,* I answer him: She can, she can!
> and the proof . . . I will make known later.

Aris also plays a supportive role in expounding the author's prime sentimental values. Remarking, "Julia proved by her own example that the flightiness of a young woman can at times be the veil or screen for the greatest virtues," the author puts his readers in the proper frame of mind to receive Aris's "spontaneous" remark to Julia: "You only had to feel once the value of true love, the value of virtue, to right yourself and despise vice."

Karamzin's approach to character production in "Julia" suggests the beginning of a new direction in his prose. As has been pointed out above, Karamzin's depictions of the anomilies and problems of character psychology in part contribute to the work's didactic texture. That is, Julia's vanity and eventual despair prejudice the reader against the social milieu which encourages her in her frivolous behavior. Conversely, the delicate joys of motherhood and sweet melancholy she experiences in the country carry with them rhetorical support for the virtues of the natural life. Karamzin's analysis of her various moods often serves as springboards for her (or the intruding author's) homilies on virtue. In addition to their role in the work's pointed lessons, however, Karamzin's characters are explored as independent psychological subjects of study. Julia maintains reader interest in her own right, the first of Karamzin's creations to achieve such independence. Her adventures and mistakes, as well as her discoveries about the world and her own inner reserves of strength, verge on the self-sustaining. Her despair at having ruined her marriage is valid beyond the didactic parallels between her and the heroine of Marmontel's "L'Heureux Divorce".[28] inherent in the story. Her gradual discovery of a new purpose in life (first in her pregnancy and then in her devotion to rearing the child) is something more than an advertisement for Rousseau's philosophy of natural education.

Julia's psychological development is an involved one as she moves from light-minded enchantress to wife to extramarital entanglements to mature mother. She lives through dilemmas and personal trauma ranging from disappointed love to near adultery, to loneliness, to resignation. She rises to marital bliss, falls into error, and finally rights herself having made important discoveries about life and her own personal relationships. *Fabula* time covers about seven years, periodically punctuated by Karamzin's description of intense psychological states of mind in the main characters (often the product of their competing strong desires). In short, the portrait Karamzin draws of his heroine is a rounded one which chronicles the stages of her personal development. Each stage of her life carries with it new problems and lessons that convey a sense of Julia's inner growth and maturation.

Julia's psychological portrait (as well as that of Aris to a lesser extent) is very much the product of Karamzin's manipulation and coordination of narrative points of view. Particularly interesting is Karamzin's reliance on editorial omniscience to create the impression of psychological depth in the characters. Using his auctorial privileges in a new way, Karamzin guides the reader into an acquaintance with the often contradictory tendencies of his characters' inner selves. Through the organizing authority of editorial omniscience he periodically ranges into the heroine's complex psyche, describing her motives and problems as well as explaining how she handles them. In the process Karamzin, speaking as intruding author, assumes a direct part in establishing her identity beyond the work's didactic themes.

Describing Julia at her flirtatious best in Moscow society he says she was quite taken with herself: *"She thought* [that she was the most beautiful], I beg you to note; but *she did not show it."* Paying the price of her foolishness in loneliness, Julia learns she is pregnant. The intruding author orients his readers to her conflicting emotions at the discovery: "Soon Julia found that she was pregnant: a new, strong feeling shook her soul! . . . joyful or mournful? . . . Julia herself could not make sense of her ideas for some time." His lucid dissection and reliable explanation of her secret feelings and thoughts reminds us of his superior vantage point as author in describing her psyche. When Julia and Aris are reunited, Karamzin relies on the unrestricted perspicacity of intruding author, creating in the process a classic example of *apophasis:*

I know the weakness of my pen and, for that

reason, I will not say anything more about this unusual development; not a word about their first exclamations that spontaneously flew from the depths of the heart; not a word about the eloquent silence of the first minutes; not a word about the tears of joy and happiness! . . .

As intruding author, Karamzin's unlimited access to character psychology extends to Aris as well. Early in the story, when he finds that Julia prefers the company of Prince N. to his own, Aris is hurt. The intruding author takes it upon himself to explain how the feeling manifests itself in the character together with a bit of his own omniscient advice:

Poor Aris! Imagine. You could have been happy, but the moment has passed! What is there to do? Withdraw. He did exactly that; it is not necessary to mention with what feeling. — Let us leave him. — Let him cry awhile in solitude and, if possible, forget the dear featherbrain.

Disappointment is repeated for Aris later as he finds Julia, now his wife, in a rendezvous with the same Prince N. Aris is once more shocked, once more unsure of what to do. The intruding author again digresses to interpose a sense of order in Aris' competing feelings:

Let each [of you] imagine himself in the place of poor Aris!. . . What was to be done? Stab them with the same dagger, quench the thirst of just revenge with blood and then . . . Kill himself as well . . . No! Aris struggled with himself — not longer than a minute; it was a terrible minute —

but he stilled his boiling heart, and disappeared!

In keeping with the generalizing tendencies of the editorial omniscient mode, Karamzin at times approaches the questions of psychology in terms of principles, applicable to whole groups. Even though Julia is popular at the beginning of the story, the intruding author assures us that she, like all people, is not totally self sufficient:

> No matter how you adore yourself; no matter how you admire your own worth — it is not enough! One must love something apart from the magical letter 'I'.

Karamzin then narrows his vision to the limits of his tale and explains how Julia started to seek someone special to love.

In explaining the unseen psychic mechanism that insures one man's popularity over that of another, the commenting author opines:

> No wonder — the heated imagination is a micro- scope which magnifies everything a thousand, a million times — and people can as stubbornly search for wit where it does not exist as they can at times wish not to see it when it is there.

The author builds on Julia's overreaction to Prince N.'s cavalier treatment of her. When she responds by hating all men, he digresses on the general problem of thinking clearly when personally distressed:

> It is forgivable; but is it fair? Are the hearts of all men cast in a single mold? Can all answer for

[the conduct of] one? . . . But a person in the
throes of his passion is a poor logician: *one*
seems to him *all,* and *all* seems like *one.*

As in most of the stories in the first group (the
notable exception being "Poor Liza") the narrator in
"Julia" is ancillary to the directive presence of editorial
omniscience. Karamzin assumes the role of finite personality only twice, and then but briefly. In both cases the
narrator enhances a moment of psychological stress in the
main characters. The first instance occurs early in the story
during Julia's described infatuation with prince N. She
finds it difficult to fend off his amorous advances and the
narrator mingles his own feelings of apprehension with
those the heroine experiences: "My own heart beats so
strongly when I imagine similar situations . . . Perhaps
some dark memories . . . Enough − ." The second time
Karamzin employs the narrator he lends a thin veil of
verisimilitude to the emotional events he describes. In an
attempt to fix the illusion that Aris actually witnessed
Julia's and the Prince's rendezvous, Karamzin clumsily
refers to a stranger who happened by at the time and then
told the narrator what he saw: "A man who saw [Aris]
leaving the path told me that his [Aris'] face was white as
a sheet, that his legs were noticeably unsteady; . . . " It is
one of the rare occasions in which the Russian forces his
material.

"Julia" represents a move in Karamzin toward more
mature romantic considerations. Gone are the facile
problems of "Natalia" and "The Beautiful Princess." The
thematics of didacticism are still salient, but Karamzin fills
out his characters in terms of their spiritual and psychic
potential. They are no longer uni-dimensional extensions
of one or another sentimental assumption. Julia's internal

complications are unique and suggest esthetic satisfaction beyond the sentimental moralism they serve. For the first time Karamzin accomplishes an organic synthesis of theme and character: Julia's problems and the solutions she finds point up the sentimental lessons of natural morality; at the same time, her mistakes and her final reward enhance her as a rounded and growing personality.

Sipovsky discusses Karamzin's prose in terms of what he calls its "new moralism," [29] suggesting that it veils a strong didactic impulse behind the emotional appeal of "touching" narrative situations. Optimism, derived from Karamzin's confidence that the "new moralism" was achievable by his Russian readers, is especially applicable to the early tales discussed here. The choice of narrative structure in those works bears ample evidence of that confidence. In each, Karamzin assumes direct control over the reader's perception and interpretation of fabula events. Through editorial omniscience he takes it upon himself to order and clarify those events for a full appreciation of the stories entails contemplation of ideals which transcend the narrative itself. The result is the reader's sense of security which marks these tales. As in the general eighteenth-century use of authorial opinion-making, Karamzin uses its privilege, often leavened with humor, to teach his audience what is right and wrong, which character is worthy of sympathy, what values are to be emulated, what each tale should teach the reader concerning the new standards of sentimental faith.

The intruding author is the axis about which Karamzin constructs his narrative scheme in these stories. The narrator, initially prominent in "Poor Liza," *feels* what the intruding author *declares* to be true. In the other works of this cycle the narrator, defined here as an observing or participating personality, is hardly present at all. After Karamzin's initial experimentation with the potential of poignant feeling, he all but discards the narrator in favor of establishing more direct means of expounding sentimental values (through clear authorial opinion).

D.S. Mirsky, the eminent Russian emigré literary historian, remarks that Karamzin was "a child of the eighteenth-century" and its neo-classical penchant for system-making. The topic Mirsky is discussing is Karamzin's language reforms,[30] but the remark applies equally to the Russian's system-making in his narrative schemata which typify his early tales. Karamzin's pre-occupation with authorial argumentation for his chosen causes alternates with his exemplification of those causes, both through the work's *fabula* and through the lyrical narrator. He thus adheres closely to the classical rhetorical model of shifting between the general and the particular, all the while keeping to a single suasive design. Even in "Julia," with its tentative suggestions of independent psychological portraiture, Karamzin's editorial opinions still determine the reader's angle of view on the heroine's inner complications. Karamzin may strike off in a new direction in exploring character psychology, but he keeps to his pattern of filtering prominent value judgments in the work through the commanding consciousness of the interpretive editor.

There is a golden thread of optimism and hope that runs through Karamzin's early tales. Those qualities are the result of his clear and positive interpretation of what each tale ultimately *means*. Whether it be "Poor Liza" or "Natalia," fairy tale or society tale, Karamzin imbues his early prose with the sense that events and problems are not isolated or accidental. They transpire within a framework of universal principles which are both knowable (with the intervening help of the commenting author) and part of a consistent value system (derived from basic sentimental beliefs). Tragedy is mitigated by hope (Liza's despair which results in her suicide is softened by authorial faith in a reconciliation in the after life). True love overcomes social obstacles (in "Natalia" and "The Beautiful Princess"). The individual can learn from his mistakes, wiping clean his past of immorality by acquiring firsthand knowledge of virtue (in "Julia"). Taken as a whole, the early stories provide a composite statement that life is stable and essentially beneficent toward man. Problems are solvable, errors can be rectified, man can hope for an inner harmony, reflective of the greater moral stability which Karamzin attributes to existence generally.

3

The Second Group of Tales:

The Decline of Hope

Karamzin's second cycle of tales ("Bornholm Island," "Sierra Morena," and "My Confession") represents a distinct contrast to the first group. In these later works there appears a marked and progressive dissolution of that faith in a stable life, based on sentimental ideals, which typified the earlier stories. The newer characters are subject to a welter of unpredictable and hostile situations which they find difficult to understand and impossible to control. Here Karamzin either suspends his earlier vision of moral stability or substitutes in its place the contemplation of forces in life, associated with fate, which destroy man's hopes with increasing malevolence. Personal virtue is no longer a reliable path to happiness. The fact that characters love one another truly no longer shields them from unanswerable disappointment in life. In one case a character remains morally unrejuvenated, and unpunished, to the very end of the story without hint of any moral consciousness.

The pronounced sense of moral relativism in Karamzin's second group of tales makes them more romantic than sentimental. The characters' choices are as individualized as their emotional states and their bizarre experiences. The reader necessarily becomes involved with the characters primarily through those experiences and thereby shares their sense of disjointedness. The emotional perturbation so prominent in these tales does not lead to any heightened understanding of life's goals but rather develops a sense of personal isolation and anxiety. The results are dire for Karamzin's characters. Their minds and spirits become agitated as they find no guiding principles in life. They fall prey to unbalanced and pessimistic interpretations of existence itself. Their failure to discover meaningful rules to live by breeds a profound restlessness which mounts with the agitating events of their lives. Nature, which earlier was man's truest moral guide in life (e.g., in "Natalia" or "Julia") now reflects his mutable, even precarious, existence. The physical world, like the characters themselves, is kinetic, given to quick and unpredictable changes. There results a new criterion of intensity as the measure of a character's experiences. In the growing moral vacuum of this period, that which is deeply stirring becomes valid in and of itself, without reference to any developed system of values in a given work. Karamzin invests these tales with a sense of fortuitous dissolution, both in terms of his individual characters, and in metaphysical speculations about the constitution of life itself.

Karamzin's transition in *Weltanschauung* is intimately linked to his choice of narrative design. As was pointed out in the preceding chapter, the positive quality of the early tales relies largely on the intruding author and his penchant for generalized explanations. Characters served more or less as his schematized examples of the very principles he declared both immutable and beneficient for all who choose to live by them. When a narrator was present, his emotional reactions and personal associations were carefully subordinated to exemplifying general moral truths which were most clearly discussed, even codified, by the intruding author. In the second group of tales the narrative task is almost wholly the responsibility of narrators who are themselves bound up emotionally in the specific situations they describe, either as observers of those events or as active participants in them. The limited knowledge and imperfect control inherent in the narrator device thus complements the relativistic, anxious quality so prominent in Karamzin's thematics. The narrator brings his reader into close emotional contact with each tale's melancholy events, but there is no longer an omniscient author to explain to his "dear reader" what general truth is to be learned from the work. The narrator's subjective involvement in the events he relates occupies the center of each tale in this cycle and he sustains an emotional tone not met before in Karamzin's prose. The adventures he describes are consistently unhappy in their results and produce a corresponding psychic movement in him from hopeful expectation to unremitting despair. His powers of vision and understanding function only to develop an emotional response to those adventures. In the last tale of this cycle ("My Confession") the narrator's response is one of flagrant cynicism, a final expression of the overall sense of life's moral disorder which builds in this group of tales.

Information concerning Karamzin's biography indicates that he went through a trying period in his life in the mid 1790's, coinciding with the publication of the stories discussed here. His correspondence of the time suggests a deep sense of personal loneliness and lack of purpose in life. Financial reversals and ill health, together with various literary quarrels, depressed him and contributed to feelings of anxiety about the premature advance of middle age. His private anxiety, a recurrent subject in letters to his close friend Dmitriev, was only deepened by his shock at the lost ideals of the French Revolution during the Robespierrean dictatorship (e.g., in his letter of August, 1793 to the same Dmitriev). [1] As G. Makogonenko stresses in his critical introduction to Karamzin's writings, Europe's decline of spiritual confidence accentuated the Russian's private despair and further slowed his already faltering faith in life's meaning. [2]

Karamzin's incidental writings of the time emphasize the same disenchantment on the public and private levels alike. "Afinskaja žizn' " ["Athenian Life"] (1793) is full of nostalgic praise for the distant past of Greece's Golden Age. To this pleasant reverie he juxtaposes the harshness and unanswerable turmoil of the present. The author's tribute to his close friend Petrov upon the latter's death, "Cvetok na grob moego Agatona" ["Flower on the Grave of My Agathon"] (1793), bears its own message on the theme of life's mutability and fleeting happiness. His "Melodor k Filaletu" ["From Melodor to Filalet"] (1793) is similarly autobiographical in its pessimistic vision, projecting a wide variety of images of optimism turning to disappointment. Taking the broad view, Melodor sees civilizations throughout time arising only to wither and disappear. The implication is that that historical process is still operative in the case of the Enlightenment. The eighteenth century with its intellectual pride, founded on spiritual optimism and the growth of science, ends in bloody repression. Speaking personally, Melodor, more than a little like Karamzin himself, feels like a man who falls asleep, seemingly secure in his home. When he awakens his familiar safety is rudely exchanged for the plains of Africa and he is beset by wild animals and the hostile elements.

"BORNHOLM ISLAND"

"Ostrov Borngol'm" ["Bornholm Island"] [3] (1794) is an account of the narrator's sea voyage from England through the Baltic Sea. At the very outset of his trip he, along with the ship's captain, stops at Gravesend on the Thames. During their short stay on land they see a young man in whose eyes "there shone the last ray of expiring life." The young stranger sings a song that bears many mysterious references to some tragic love affair and the island of Bornholm. The stranger is obviously suffering the last pangs of an impossible love and the narrator responds with genuine sympathy. However, before he can learn the exact nature of the unfortunate man's story, the captain informs him that they must return to the ship.

The mystery does not fade from the narrator's mind and when by chance they stop at Bornholm, an "awesome" *[groznyj]* place, he decides to explore it in the hope of learning its secret. After a description of the wild landscape, the narrator finds his way by chance to a mysterious castle. Prodded by curiosity and gaining admittance by the age-old rule of hospitality he succeeds in spending the night within its walls. Inside, the castle only fires his imagination the more with its Gothic scenes of ruin and decay. The master of the castle fits the Ossianic atmosphere as he gives the narrator a brief history of the violent, pagan traditions of the place.

Retiring for the night the narrator is disturbed by violent dreams in which medieval warriors attack him and a fabulous monster descends upon him. Awakening, he wanders in the garden and discovers a secret dungeon beneath the castle. In it a beautiful girl is held captive and is, like the young man met earlier, breathing her last. Her cryptic references to love and some terrible transgression also refer back to the young man and it is apparent they were lovers before their separation. Like her male counterpart, the girl inspires the narrator's faith and sympathy; but the story-teller is equally unsuccessful in ascertaining the nature of her dilemma. The girl refuses to talk and the narrator is forced to leave her to her cruel fate.

Awakened the next morning by his host, the narrator finally learns the secret of the two lovers. It is unclear, but the master of the castle is apparently the girl's father. However, as the narrator enticingly explains to the reader, the secret of the two lovers is so shocking that he refuses to write about it, at least in this story. The narrator makes his return to the ship and leaves the island, very much disturbed, but still uncommunicative as to what exactly constitutes the tragic love and why the young couple was so cruelly punished.

The implication is that their relationship was incestuous. The indirect appearance of such a taboo in Russian literature, and the agitating effect of leaving the story apparently unended, certainly achieved Karamzin's provacative intent. Even though he never thought of continuing the work, critics and readers alike waited for its sequel. When none appeared there were more than a few piqued tempers among Karamzin's most loyal admirers.

The enigma of the unsuccessful lovers is hardly enough to maintain the story's compositional coherence. The narrator, through his rich gifts of lyricism, builds the scanty facts of the tale into an extensive chain of subjective associations, moody nature descriptions, and personal speculations on what he learns about life. The rhythm of his swelling subjectivity does more than accentuate his adventures. His agitated thoughts and personalized descriptions organize those events into the overall production of his private tone poem. The work is a chronicle of the narrator's changing world view as much as it is a recounting of events in other people's lives. In this Karamzin provides an early Russian example of the growing European interest in what Karl Kroeber, the contemporary American critic, calls "narrative lyricism," one of the most sturdy and characteristic features of growing romanticism in the West. [4] The narrator's perception of places and characters, his subjective descriptions of locale, and the general direction of his accumulated moods, combine to constitute the compositional center of the work. *Fabula* events serve as a convenient narrative frame on which Karamzin, through his narrator, weaves the work's lyrical cloth.

The component parts of Karamzin's tone poem in prose are, first, the narrator's intimacy and his general tendency to conjure associations between what he sees and his own fertile imagination. Second, Karamzin orchestrates his narrator's subjective moods with numerous nature descriptions. These reinforce his moods and heighten their emotional potential. Third, the motif of the narrator's sea voyage itself, with its alternation between the safety of the ship and the hostile power of the sea, serves to restate poetically the central theme of the work. On each of these levels Karamzin develops several examples of a single movement from hopefulness to gloom. These accumulate and develop into a consistent statement on the theme of life's instability.

Throughout the tale Karamzin creates a rich background of semantically suggested parallels, euphonic accentuations, and imagery (auditory and visual) which obliquely maintain the atmosphere of muffled despair. The opening lines of the story suggest its lyrical direction:

> Druz'ja! prošlo krasnoe leto, zlataja osen' poblednela, zelen' uvjala, dereva stojat bez plodov i bez list'ev, tumannoe nebo volnuetsja, kak mračnoe more, zimnij pux sypletsja na xladnuju zemlju — prostimsja s prirodoju do radostnogo vesennego svidanija, ukroemsja ot v'jug i metelej — ukroemsja v tixom kabinete svoem!

> [Friends! beautiful summer has passed, golden autumn has paled, greenery has wilted, trees stand without their fruits, without leaves, the hazy sky is agitated like the gloomy sea, and winter's down scatters on the cold earth. Let us bid farewell to nature until its joyful return in the spring, let us seek shelter in our quiet study!]

The mesmeric repetition of back vowels and the rhythmical sequence of short clauses induce a sense of detachment from the physical world of the commonplace. It sensitizes the reader to the nuances of rhythm and suggestion which dominate the narrative.

At the beginning of his trip, the narrator stops by chance at Gravesend. His description of the place contains the characteristic alternation between positive and negative suggestion which permeates the story. Nature at first appears to him in a positive light. The green fields are "decorated by nature and man's diligence;" his vision is one of "rare and picturesque places." The picture is then altered, however, for the narrator also views the sea which bombards Gravesend from the "gloomy distance" with a "hollow roar" and a "doleful noise." The seascape is chaotic, lacking in that good order which characterizes man's more reasonable industry in the fields. That basic tension between the sea's unbridled power and the more delicate aspects of human planning acts as a musical motif, periodically punctuating both narrative and descriptive passages in the tale. Here, the sea inspires a tenuous association with death in the narrator. It evokes a dream-like state which, as he explains, "is the most expressive and most poetic image of death."

The movement towards death in the narrator's description of nature and his own reverie are preparatory to Karamzin's introduction of the mysterious youth whom he meets at Gravesend. There follows immediately the first of several ties between the narrator's lyrical mood and the tale's sparse events. The stranger's song amplifies death through its reference to some unexplained tragedy which has destroyed his life, together with that of a mysterious girl who lives on Bornholm Island. He ends his song with a suggestion of his own suicide by drowning, again an indirect link between the sea and man's unhappy condition.

The narrator is forced to leave Gravesend just as he is about to speak to the stranger. His return to the ship and his departure are marked by an expressive lyrical moment in which he internalizes his experiences, giving them subjective form. The sea's hostility is present through the suggestive references to birds which at first follow the ship as it sails out to sea. They soon return to shore, however, "as if they were terrified by the vastness of the sea." Then the narrator repeats the attribute "terrified" *(ustrašennyj)* in rendering his own mood while gazing at the water: "The agitation of the noisy waters and the hazy sky remained the only subject for our eyes, a subject grandiose and terrible *(strašnyj)*."

Experience has not yet dampened his native optimism for he can still take pride in man's ability to control his own destiny. The ship is his focus for that optimism and, as he commends its ability to overcome the dangers of the ocean, he sings the praises of man who dares to travel *"where one thin board,"* as Wieland says, *"separates us from a watery death."* He expands on that hopeful faith with the remark *"Nil mortalibus arduum est* ('There is nothing impossible for mortals')." His ruminations on hope mark a high point of optimism which begins the swift downward slide of his faith, as later events and his lyrical responses are to prove.

After an attack of sea-sickness the narrator finds the ship in smooth water and safe. His impressions and private thoughts are mixed. With his recovery from illness he experiences a rush of vigor which is bound up with his positive attitude toward nature. The sky is clear, the water is radiant with the sun's golden rays and there is a panorama of colorful flags, blue and rose-colored, of other ships enjoying the placid weather. The ship, that perennial reminder of man's faith in bending the sea's power to his own rational design, cuts through the waves "which vainly try to outstrip it." On learning that they are approaching Bornholm, however, the narrator's mood changes immediately. The captain informs him that the place is "dangerous for ships; there are shoals and rocks hidden on the sea's bottom." These topographical details take on suggestive value for the human situation when the narrator allows his imagination to return to the young man at Gravesend whose song full of "sad notes and words" complement Bornholm's melancholy physical appearance.

Picking up the key word "terrifying," appropriate to his earlier thoughts about the sea, the narrator applies it to the island: "It seemed inaccessible from all sides, barred all around by the hand of grandiose nature. Only that which was terrifying *[strašnyj]* was evident on its grey cliffs." The suggested presence of a hostile force extending from the sea to the island is thus accomplished. Working deeper into his ominous associations he meditates on thoughts of death which are involuntarily suggested by the island's forbidding appearance: "With horror I saw there the image of cold, silent eternity, the image of implacable death. . ." At that point nature's hostile posture toward man suggests to the narrator the secret which binds the stranger at Gravesend to Bornholm. He thereby transposes fully into the human realm a mood which he has carefully constructed in the context of nature.

Moving inland, the narrator repeats his characteristic inner transition from a positive to a negative view of his surroundings. His initial impression is one of well-tended fields, neat homes and a colorful sunset. The harmony between nature and man's use of the land for his own advantage (i.e., the well-tended fields) echoes his first impression of Gravesend. Spying a castle he moves closer to it. As he does so there occurs again the transition in mood from cheerful to gloomy thoughts. Nature turns more threatening with the fading light, as it did earlier: "Silence reigned over all, in the distance the sea pounded, the last ray of evening's light was expiring *[ugasal]* on the bronze spires of the [castle's] towers." The phrase *poslednij luč večernego sveta ugasal* brings to mind his morbid description of the youth at Gravesend. In his eyes there also *sijal poslednij luč ugasajuščej zizni.* The narrator sustains his active imagination as he comes to the gates of the castle. He compares his guide, who is afraid of the strange place, to a prisoner at the moment of his execution, thereby picking up the nuance of death in nature mentioned just before (i.e., expiring light). The impressions of nature, the past events of the story, and the narrator's subjective associations, are starting to weave an intricate and varied design of images of how life shades into death.

The next stage of the story takes place inside the castle as the host tells the narrator of his life on the island as well as of the island's history. His is a secondary narration within the story proper, but it too is characterized by the same aura of pessimism and contributes to the work's overall mood. He speaks of his "dying heart;" the narrator describes his "gloomy visage," which puts him in mind of "sorrowful winter." The basic link between melancholy features in both man and nature is thus formed here as elsewhere in the story. The old host is an Ossianic figure who relates the history of his people in terms of their bloody sacrifices to pagan idols, its perverted customs and "discordant songs." His conversations with the story teller also strike the main note of false optimism. The host asks about intellectual and moral progress in the outside world. The narrator is forced to reply that, although science and its application are spreading, "human blood still streams on the earth, the tears of the miserable still flow, the name of virtue is applauded but men disagree over its substance." The host's response is only a knowing shrug, as if he fully expected it to be so.

There is a strong Gothic quality to the narrator's overnight stay in the castle which Karamzin effectively incorporates into the general context of betrayed hope. Auditory imagery of hollow footsteps, metal clanking on stone, steel doors banging and sending their ominous echoes resounding through the castle, accentuate the already rich pall of suggested gloom in the tale. Visual images of broken columns, discarded artifacts and ill-preserved art also convey the idea of melancholy. Given his penchant for comparing the sights he encounters with aspects of death, the narrator draws a simile between his observations in the castle and a graveyard. The scenes of ruin in the building itself, together with the aura of spiritual decay in the island's history and the host's own somber life, remind him of gravestones and the dust of the departed. As he often does, he establishes connections between one melancholy situation in the tale and earlier sights or experiences, thereby maintaining the melodically repetitive structure of the work. Amidst his morose thoughts, "the image of the sad stranger on Gravesend arose in my soul and I fell asleep." The tenuous web of memory and echoed events moves through the piece like a recurrent musical refrain in a minor key, constantly leading the reader into a lyrically suggested confrontation with the central issue of hopelessness.

The consistency of the narrator's lyrical ordering of events is attested to by his handling of the dreams that disturb his rest. He at first finds it hard to sleep. When he does, his unwholesome nightmares echo the pervasive theme of violent nature and the implicit metaphor of danger to man's well-being. In this case, he puts into the apparition's speech a syntactic parallel between Bornholm's danger to seafarers ("Do sailors not turn pale at the sight of its granite shores?") and the fearful dangers the castle holds for the narrator ("Does the traveler not run away from its menacing towers?"). The effect is that of further strengthening the already clear relation between the sea's dangers and the peril that hangs over human affairs on the island.

Morose moods follow one another quickly for the narrator. At the same time, he is given to fewer and fewer positive descriptions of nature or positive private thoughts. The tide of suggested despondency is running more quickly. Venturing into a secret garden after his agitated sleep he at first finds nature calm and almost soothing: "The night was bright, the light of the full moon silvered the dark greenery of the old oaks and elms." But, against the persistent presence of the muffled ocean, that constant reminder of danger and inconstancy in life, the narrator wanders into the dark paths of the garden, leaving behind the pale hopefulness of the moon. His psyche undergoes the regular pattern of turning to gloomy thoughts as ideas of ancient secrets, Druids and all the terrors of their religious ceremonies beset him.

This inner shift from buoyancy to thoughts of death, by now a commonplace, occurs immediately prior to his accidental meeting with the girl held prisoner beneath the castle. She, like her male counterpart at Gravesend, is near death with no hope to keep her alive. The narrator's response to each is one of intuitive sympathy; he is convinced in each case that the sufferer is pursued by an unjust fate. To complete the symmetry of the two encounters, the narrator fails to learn why the girl is being punished, as he did with the youth earlier. She speaks only in vague terms of breaking some solemn commandment; the young man earlier referred in his song to the same kind of transgression. The fact that the two meetings bracket the main events of the tale and are marked by numerous parallels to one another increase the lyrical quality of the work's composition. The transition in mood from hope to despair which has already been accomplished in each character, together with the same gradual transition in the narrator, provide highly visible points of reference in the work that vary and repeat the same issue throughout the piece.

A high point in the narrator's experience on Bornholm occurs after his interview with the girl, as he tries to determine what he has learned of life in the course of his bizarre adventures. He expresses a clear acknowledgment of the very rhythm of hope turning to despair which has periodically obtruded in the story. Cataloging the apparent blessings of nature, the narrator at first summarizes his own hoped-for stability in life: " 'My God!, I thought, 'My God!' How sad it is to be excluded from the society of the living, free, joyful creatures which populate the boundless expanses of nature!" He tries to evoke the faith he once had that nature is beneficent toward man and might relieve him of his burden of disappointment. His thought is echoed by a melodic repetition of "and here" *[i zdes']* as he lists nature's positive aspects. All is in vain, however, and with the caesura-like interjection "But" *[No]* he proceeds to deny that false optimism by listing nature's failures to help the girl:

> But — the poor girl, locked in a dungeon, does not have this consolation [of nature] : the morning dew does not sprinkle her languid heart, the breeze does not refresh her exhausted breast, the sun's rays do not illumine her clouded eyes, the tender balsamic outpourings of the moon do not nourish her soul with gentle dreams and pleasant thoughts.

The insistent rhythm of negated verbs serves as a musical counterpoint to the optimistic hope of the earlier repetition of "and here" in the same paragraph. The final acknowledgment of life's instability, the suggestion of which has been accumulating throughout the tale, finds a final resolute expression in the narrator's rhetorical exclamation "Creator! Why have you given men the destructive power to make themselves and one another unhappy?"

The narrator's final despair contrasts sharply with his attitude as he sets out on his voyage. There, his key phrase is *"Nil mortalibus arduum est."* His reference to the ship and its "thin board separating man from a watery death" is a high point of faith. His trip over the ocean is a metaphor of his developing experience with life's reality.[5] The voyage leads him to the hostile shores of Bornholm and his increased acquaintance with life leads him to a sense of unmitigated pessimism. To pursue the basic metaphor of the work, the thin board of optimism that protected him from the ocean — life's hostility — has broken. He is engulfed by the terrible *(strašnyj)* fear that life is unbalanced and dangerous.

The effectiveness of the narrator's account of faith's dissolution in the course of his adventures is greatly enhanced by his refusal to explain what he learns about the lovers from his host. It is, he says, too disturbing and painful for him to discuss. The secret not only piques the reader's curiosity but also drives home once more the fact that there is no explaining consciousness in the story. The narrator portrays his own distraught response to the pitfalls of life but he cannot square them with any overall purpose or meaning. The reader's feelings of disquiet at the unsolved enigma create in him a sense of helpless disorder which besets the narrator to a far greater degree. The ending is thus consistent, both with the basic theme of instability, and with the emotional perspective and limited cognition implicit in the narrator's point of view.

The narrator's short prologue to his tale represents

his new attitude inspired by his unhappy experiences on "the sea of life." Its references to the passage of beautiful summer and the advent of bleak autumn with its withering of greenery, capture the mood of blighted optimism which underpins the composition of the tale in its entirety. The motif of the sea is also present as a somber echo of its symbolic role in the events of the work as he compares the autumnal sky to a "gloomy sea." The narrator's reaction to existence in the prologue is best described as Epicurean in the sense of renouncing all attempts to interact with life or seek its change according to any reasonable design of his own. Like his ancient predecessors in the philosophy of personal withdrawal, the narrator seeks to cultivate his own modest pleasures in his "quiet study" whenever possible, out of the reach of cruel reality. The passivity and introversion he evinces here find adequate explanation in his growing despondency as he describes it in the tale. The final expression of that despondency, placed at the beginning of the work, thus contributes to the suggestive fabric of the entire piece.

The lyrical composition of "Bornholm Island" concentrates the reader's attention primarily on the evolution of the narrator's subjective view of life. He is an emotional presence in the story, and his ordering of events and descriptions reflects the alteration of his own vision. That change is delicately chronicled in his growing disenchantment with hope and the increasing evidence of some hostile force in life which defeats man at each turn (e.g., in the lovers he meets singly, the master of the castle as well as his own perception of nature's mutability and the incessant symbol of the sea's dark power).

As the sole narrative perspective in this tale, the unsettled narrator projects an imperfect and subjective set of attitudes onto what he relates. As the only source of narration, his field of vision is so closely bound to the events he describes that he cannot see beyond them. He can only respond to them emotionally. The story is more concerned in the final analysis with his subtle psychological changes in cognition than with the sparse *fabula* events of mysterious lovers and Gothic castles. Those events function as a convenient background against which the narrator's rhythmical movement toward despair assumes form. There results a sense of personal agitation on his part which, as it coalesces with kinetic forces in nature, forms a uniformly unstable, threatened atmosphere in the tale. It is the creation of that delicately shaded mood, on all its levels, which spells the tale's real worth. There is a nearly perfect union of theme, narrative perspective, and compositional structure which reveal Karamzin's prodigious talent and sensitivity to the narrative task.

"SIERRA MORENA"

"Sierra-Morena" ["Sierra Morena"] [6] (1795) treats even more violent aspects of unreliable life than appear in "Bornholm Island." It is a much shorter story than its predecessor and lacks its richness in variation and delicacy of lyricism. "Sierra Morena" is a more intense work and explores the rude juxtaposition of personal hope and despair as no previous work by Karamzin has. The metaphorical expression of those human extremes which he develops in nature continues to point up the work's emotional tension, as in "Bornholm Island," but the metaphor here is more concentrated and more violent. In concert with a heightened exhibition of man's misery in life, Karamzin brings his narrator into more intimate involvement with the events he describes. Instead of observing events externally from a position of mere sympathy, as was the case in "Bornholm Island," the narrator in "Sierra Morena" is the main protagonist of the work. His increased personal stake in the outcome of his own adventures correspondingly increases his inner tension as he relates the story; there is no emotional distance for him as he observes the events he describes. He is strictly limited by his own experiences as he tries to arrive at, first a cognition and, then, an interpretation of what happens to him. With the suspension of all other avenues of information gathering within the narrative process, Karamzin provides a most effective mode for portraying issues of anxiety and relativism.

The *fabula* of "Sierra Morena" again treats the question of love. As in "Bornholm Island," however, it is a love against which the flow of life exerts a hostile strength which is overwhelming.[7] The narrator falls in love with the heroine, Elvira, who lives in Andalusia. Elvira has pledged her love, however, to another man, Alonzo. Alonzo has apparently been lost at sea but Elvira remains constant to his memory and refuses all other romantic attachments. The narrator at first limits his attentions to brotherly consolation, and finds that Elvira returns his feeling warmly. They are inseparable in their lament for Alonzo, but the relationship grows despite their intentions and the narrator declares his love for her. Surprised by his ardor, as well as by her own responsiveness, Elvira agrees to marry him. Their decision to live for the future rather than for obligations to the past at first spells great promise for their honest love. At the very marriage altar, however, Alonzo makes his sudden appearance. He had just escaped from imprisonment at the hands of Algerian pirates who had earlier taken him from his wrecked ship. Interpreting Elvira's impending marriage as a mark of her inconstancy,

Alonzo punishes her by committing suicide at the moment of her marriage.

The slide towards total destruction increases rapidly as Elvira refuses to say her marriage vows and renounces her worldly life by entering a strict nunnery. The narrator's shock at the suicide and at Elvira's refusal to even speak to him quickly destroy his basic optimism. He wanders about the world disconsolate, everywhere meeting signs of the futility of society and of life itself. Those who had wished the narrator well in his coming marriage now perversely laugh at his ordeal. He comes to define existence as an empty and cruel joke with man as the butt. His own sad lot colors his interpretation of all life and, in an apocalyptic state of mind, he renounces identification with his debased species: "I take leave of you! Rage on in your wild frenzies; rip each other apart, destroy one another! My heart is dead to you and your fate does not touch me." His death-like alternative to wasted hope is all that remains constant and real for him and he waits patiently for his life to end.

"Sierra Morena," like "Bornholm Island," maintains Karamzin's interest in a plot built around the narrator's movement from hope to despair within a context of physical love. The essential compositional structure, as in "Bornholm Island," is still a chronicle of that mutation in the narrator's *Weltanschauung.* The movement is only quicker in its pace here and clearer in developing a sense of cosmic loneliness. The transition revolves about a single event (Alonzo's suicide) rather than developing gradually through a number of suggestive plot events as in "Bornholm Island" (e.g., the stranger's dilemma on Gravesend, the morose master of the castle and his reveries, the plight of the captive maiden, and finally the narrator's discovery of the secret of the lovers).

Again, as in "Bornholm Island," Karamzin lyrically portrays the narrator's transition from happiness to despair through the expanded metaphor of nature. Consonant with the more traumatic events and emotions of this tale, however, he creates a more turbulent landscape. The coordination of character psychology and nature begins immediately in the tale. The narrator describes the beauties of the locale in which the story takes place (Andalusia) with a series of rhythmically short clauses initiated by the word *tam* ["there"]:

> tam, gde šumjat gordye pal'my, gde blagouxajut mirtovye rošči, gde veličestvennyj Gvadal'kvivir katit medlenno svoi vody, gde vozvyšaetsja rozmarinom uvenčannaja Sierra-Morena, . . .

> [there, where the proud palms rustle, where myrtle groves scent the air, where the magnificent Guadalquiver slowly rolls its waters, where there rises Sierra-Morena, crowned with rosemary, . .]

There then follows a matching set of equally short clauses describing the beauties of the heroine, Elvira. The opening word is again *tam* ["there"], thereby suggesting the basic link between human and natural spheres:

> tam uvidel ja prekrasnuju, kogda ona v unynii, v goresti stojala podle Alonzova pamjatnika, opersis' na nego lelejnoju rukoju svoeju: . .

> [there I saw the beautiful [Elvira] as she stood next to Alonzo's monument in grief and sorrow, leaning on it with her lily-white hand; . .]

The suggested proximity of Elvira's beauty with that of nature is accomplished fully by ending the description with an intermingling of their physical qualities:

> luč utrennego solnca pozlaščal beluju urnu i vozvyšal trogatel'nye prelesti nežnoj El'viry; ee rusye volosy, rassypajas' po plečam, padali na černyj mramor.

> [a ray of the morning sun turned the white urn to gold and heightened the touching charms of the tender Elvira; her red hair, falling about her shoulders, fell on the black marble.]

As is typical of much romantic fiction, the hero projects his inner feelings onto his physical environment, seeing in nature a reflection of his own emotional condition. As his and Elvira's affection begins subtly to grow, the narrator describes natural surroundings as similarly tender: "Two sighs escaped us. Joining and mingling with a zephyr, they disappeared in the airy spaces." Subsequently their stronger feelings develop amidst the more agitated descriptions of waterfalls and resounding echoes in the rugged mountains, where "strong winds disturb and twirl the air, scarlet flashes of lightning curl against the black sky." Strong, passionate colors in nature adequately suggest the comparable strength and passion of the couple's love, described in the same paragraph. Elvira is especially drawn to the stronger moods of nature. As the hero-narrator remarks, "they exalted, delighted, and nourished her soul." The narrator is thankful to the night mists which "drew our hearts closer" and help him to sense her proximity more poignantly. Their final declaration of love takes place in the stimulating isolation prepared for them by sympathetic, even abetting nature.

In the narrator's representation of his and Elvira's mutually acknowledged love, he resorts to a host of hyperbolic images from nature to convey the full force of their emotion, much as Byron was to do twenty years later. "Ach! you can battle with your heart stubbornly and at length, but who can conquer it? The stormy course of its furious waters tears apart all obstructions, and mountains of stone collapse from the strength of the fiery substance trapped in their depths." The forced union of such violently diverse images as water and erupting lava is itself expressive of the psychological contest between diverse emotions the narrator sees in Elvira as she struggles between her vow to the "dead" Alonzo and her love for him: "Elvira turned pale — and again flushed to the color of a rose. Signs of fear, doubt, grief, tender languor played upon her face!"

Life's underlying hostility which accompanies the passion of the lovers surfaces in the image of thunder (in "Bornholm Island" it was the sea). Elvira's honest, strong feelings for the narrator induce her to renounce a commitment to the dead and live for the positive potential of the future. As she declares her love for the narrator, however, she speaks of thunder and retribution. The narrator also refers to thunder as a metaphor of gathering fate and its destruction of the true love experienced by the betrothed couple.

The extreme punishment Alonzo visits upon Elvira, the resultant shock to the couple at the altar, and their permanently broken relationship, all happen like a whirlwind which carries away all human hope and faith in life. A single grandiose juxtaposition forces the narrator to view the malevolence of life head on and his shock robs him of his finer sentiments. He ceases to expect anything good of his fellow man. Even more than the narrator of "Bornholm Island," this narrator's disappointment comes to dominate his definition of all life and leads to overtly expressed cynicism, a new posture for Karamzin: "thinking about life and death of whole peoples I actively came to feel the trivia of all existence and said to myself: 'what is human life? What is our being? One moment and everything will disappear! The smile of happiness and the tears of grief will be covered by the same clod of earth!' "

The narrator's arrival at his final cry of "nihil" over man and society also finds a restatement in nature. The flowering luxury of Spain, traditionally linked to human passion, is associated with his happy past. After his tragic confrontation with fate he exchanges all that for the "sad remains of ancient Palmyra." He wanders through its ruins, matching his burned-out soul with its decayed remnants of a better past. As the narrator closes his tale he explains that he chooses to live in the north, where he can merge his own sense of emptiness with the larger vacuum of nature's barrenness, calming his sick spirit with thoughts of eternal nothingness. He "listens to the deep, eloquent silence which reigns in this desolation. . ." The only sound is that of thunder, that reminder of life's cruel treatment of man's frail hopes. Since his own soul is dead, he seeks out an appropriate natural setting in which to drag out the rest of his days "where out of its uncaring depths majestic nature has accepted me into its embraces and has included me in its system of *ephemeral* existence — I live in solitude and listen to storms." The narrator once extended himself towards human warmth. It is to a repository of death in nature that he now offers himself: "Silent night — eternal silence — sacred stillness. To you I hold out my embraces!"

Karamzin's presentation of life's precariousness finds an increasingly powerful mode of expression in his choice of narrator. For the romantic narrator, his opinions on life in general proceed directly from what he personally experiences and feels. He has only the events of his own life to guide him and he is emotionally absorbed in them. Since his own experiences are traumatic, his entire world view is necessarily pessimistic. Personal disillusionment breeds a sense of such introversion in him that it excludes everything in his life not directly related to that central issue. There results, then, a complete reversal of roles in the narrator from that evident in the intruding author of the earlier tales. The narrator views all life through the magnifying lens of his own feelings. For him the particular determines the significance of the whole in life.

Karamzin's exclusive concern with a narrow range of the narrator's personal considerations represents a deepening of the alienation process begun in "Bornholm Island." The more clearly defined destruction of the narrator's faith matches his more intimate involvement with his own story. These features combine to achieve the first distinct hint of the romantic revolt against life which is to later typify early nineteenth-century literary taste. The narrator of "Bornholm Island" was somewhat removed from the events he described and thereby retained some semblance of peace in life (i.e., his retreat into Epicurean passivity). This narrator has lost even that last shred of control over his despair and harbors a suggestion of rebellion which later (in "My Confession") will take on a more definite form.

"MY CONFESSION"

"Moja ispoved' " ["My Confession"] (1802) was

written when Karamzin's personal fortunes were improving and his optimism about the future was beginning to take form. Yet this hero, or more properly this anti-hero, Count N. N., presents the most pessimistic and perverse attitudes of any Karamzinian character. He successfully tramples on a wide variety of the most sacred values of personal morality, social virtue, and religious faith to be found in traditional Western culture. What is more, the hero is immune from even the slightest twinge of conscience as he sneers at great art and learning, and devastates the lives of all who come into intimate contact with him. He enjoys each adventure in corruption to its fullest potential.

"My Confession" is a product of the issues Karamzin raises in "Bornholm Island" and "Sierra Morena," (i.e. moral relativism and the limited vision of a narrator-hero). Count N. N. is the narrator of his own story and is the sole means by which the reader learns of his malignant exploits. Moreover, the Count is in many ways the only character in the story. It is impossible for him to relate to any one except as they serve as opportunities for his campaign to indulge his every caprice. Earlier narrators made strenuous attempts to establish contact with others, either through sympathy (as in "Bornholm Island") or through romantic love (as in "Sierra Morena"). Count N. N.'s world is a completely relativist one from the very beginning of the story in the sense that nothing is important to him for its own sake. He can only relate to his environment (physical, emotional, and social) by twisting it to his own purposes.

Karamzin is still fascinated here by the question of individualism but he paints the Count as its dead end when carried to an extreme. As will be discussed at greater length later, Karamzin both explores the furthest limits of the isolated ego and attempts to warn his readers about the dire results it implies. The latter aspect of the tale seems to imply his first tentative faith in the idea that the individual can have a meaningful place in society and even improve it. It is a proposal which is certainly basic to the central idea behind the *Messenger of Europe* (in which "My Confession" appeared).

There is no integrated *fabula* in "My Confession." As an autobiography the "author" subjectively selects those events from his past which he considers typical or significant of his own personality. He prides himself on the directness and brevity of his composition, unlike other writers: "I shall describe the most important events in my life on a single piece of paper." His memories are varied and cover the time from his childhood to his maturity. Yet each memory is a match with the others in that they all flaunt the cultural ideals of society which every Karamzinian hero before Count N. N. supported (in the first cycle of tales) or tried to support (in "Bornholm Island" and in "Sierra Morena"). For example, the Count describes his education as a series of falsified progress reports to his parents, prepared with the aid of his Swiss tutor, Mendel. The tutor is a perfect complement to the Count for neither takes anything seriously which does not provide self-centered pleasure. As Mendel says of the Count early in their acquaintance: "Nature and fate have conspired to make you the very image of amiability and happiness; you are handsome, intelligent, rich and of a good family. That is enough for a brilliant role in society! All the rest is not worth the trouble." The pair travels to Leipzig for the fashionable completion of the hero's education only to turn day into night and live a constant revel. To show his scorn for education the Count indulges in a series of puns on the subject to exhibit his wit. He remarks that he "wasted no time in getting acquainted with all the famous professors — and nymphs." Copying his tutor he gives "dinners for the first and for the latter — suppers." Continuing to value a good joke over formal education he jibes that as a result of his constant carousals he slept during his lectures and "could not hear enough *[naslušat'sja]* because he never listened *[ne slušal]*."

Leaving Leipzig after three years of uninterrupted irresponsibility the hero travels about Europe, paying a secretary to supply his parents with observations and descriptions which he represents as his own. Again, his behavior brings him nothing but increased fame as a perceptive and articulate traveler. The most notable experiences of his wanderings are creating scandals at balls (dropping his German dancing partners on the floor), shooting paper balls at his coachmen, and biting the Pope's foot. In Paris he polishes the intricacies of lovemaking and praises the right notables, both in government and in the literary world, with the result that everyone considers him a fine intellect and a rare talent. Here, as is the case throughout the story, the hero's selfishness and renunciation of basic standards of honesty are crowned with success and popularity.

Karamzin's image of the anti-hero is starting to take on definite form and the world in which he lives reveals a dimension of dark cynicism. It rewards his negation of an increasingly wide range of the very ideals of knowledge, love, and virtue which Karamzin had maintained throughout his writing career.

The rest of the work chronicles exploits similar to those described above. The only differences are, first, the Count's behavior becomes increasingly destructive of those who come into contact with him, and, second, he meets with ever-increasing success in the process. His exploits do not bother him a whit, for his enjoyment of each misanthropic experience constitutes the only stable factor in his life. In London he drinks himself into illness and his first act upon recovery is to draw derogatory caricatures of the royal family. He returns to his homeland bored, incapable of clear thought or strong feelings. In the relativist world in which he lives, however, there is no need for such qualities to bother him for long. His view that "all [social] rules are halters for those with weak minds, all obligations are unbearable coercion" frees him for an unlimited array of enjoyments fit for a rake. His inner vacuity results in consistent success as his manners, dress, behavior, and jaded humor inspire widespread admiration from his countrymen. His cruel treatment of women, by way of "enjoying" the delights of love, is based on the idea of inspiring a variety of guilt, fear, self-reproach, and jealousy in his female opponent. The few women who survive his premeditated campaign fall victim to his acid wit or his perverted talent as a caricaturist.

The Count reaches a new low (or, in his anti-system of values, a new high) when he marries an innocent and devoted girl only to humiliate her by his open infidelity. His cruel jokes to her on the subject are designed to prod her into a similar existence. He is only satisfied when he sees her "deliverance" from traditional moral limits: "Finally I became completely convinced of my wife's reform [his inverted term for her corruption], seeing about her a crowd of devotees. Our home was much more pleasant for it." Having successfully debauched the sanctity of his own home, it is not surprising that he is devoid of any sense of filial obligation as well. His mother laments his extravagance with money and the loose living in which he and his wife now indulge. Ignoring her entreaties, he helps hasten her death. True to his own egoism, he laments her demise only because it forces him into a short period of mourning which suspends his perpetual round of "entertainment."

Inevitable financial bankruptcy finally puts an end to the Count's riotous living. His wife disappears, he is left with no friends, and he walks the streets with his sole remaining property — two boxes of old love letters and the clothes on his back. The hero is impervious to adversity, however, because he has no external standards of behavior, conscience, or success against which to judge his condition. His only standards, after all, are novelty and physical stimulation, and his reduced position satisfies both. He had never been poor before and he had never experienced the physical sensation of hunger or the prospect of debtors' prison. With such relativist standards he avoids pitfalls, simply because the instability they create is his normality. His whole existence is a denial of predictable moral order and an acceptance of the world's basic unreliability. Indeed, the Count does emerge from his scrape successfully, even providentially. His wife has a proposal of marriage from a rich elderly prince. To gain the hero's release of his wife's marriage contract, the prince agrees to buy up the Count's debts and even take him into his home as part of the family. The first proposal costs the Count no loss of dignity (since he has none as far as society is concerned) and the second provides a new vista of opportunities for his jaded sense of humor. He readily releases his wife and moves in with the prince.

Given the Count's reprobate character, he loses no time in seducing his former wife, barely holding back his laughter as he does so. To heighten the novelty of his conquest he talks her into running away with him, thereby spicing his adventure with his host's bitter humiliation. Predictably, at this point in Karamzin's drawing of his hero, Count N. N. forces his "lover" to sell the jewels she carried away from the prince in order to support the same riotous life style they had enjoyed before. But, when she learns he has been unfaithful to her in their new relationship, she dies from total disillusionment. She says such things to him "that would have made my hair stand on end if there had been but a spark of conscience in me." True to his amoral philosophy, however, he can listen to her speech without emotion and then fall quietly asleep.

The Count's capacity to turn what is bizarre for others into something natural for himself is proved once again as he summarizes the rest of his life, up to the writing of his "confession." Being so well acquainted with vice, immorality, and debt, he decides to turn his experience to profit and becomes both a usurer and a procurer for "men and women in their little weaknesses." As always, life conspires to abet this hero; he turns vice to profit and finds ample evidence that his tastes in corruption flourish everywhere in society. He is at peace with himself and is content with the way life is arranged to shower blessings on him. He would not change one of his past deeds, he says, even if he could. He compares himself to a traveler who, "standing on a height, sweeps his gaze over the places he has traversed, and gladly remembers what had been and says to himself — thus did I live!"

Karamzin's intent behind "My Confession" was undoubtedly a highly moral one, using the hero as an example of the very attitudes he would like to expose and criticize. [9] The tale's title refers specifically to Rousseau's own *Les Confessions* (published 1781-1888) (Karamzin originally subtitled his piece "A Response to J. J. Rousseau's *Confessions"*). The fact that Count N. N. indulges in the memory of past sins brings to mind the Frenchman's own self-castigation for milder offenses against God and decency. The master confessionist extolled virtue directly while Karamzin indirectly sought the same end by the rhetorical device of negative example.

Karamzin saw in the Count the representative of a type which he considered all too common in Russia of the late eighteenth century. At the beginning of the story he pridefully lists his unique "qualities" (i.e., the most glaring faults of his early character and education). These coincide with those typical problems of the Russian aristocracy of that day: "I was born the son of a rich, illustrious land-owner — and grew up to be a clown! I committed all kinds of nasty pranks — and was never punished! I learned French — and knew nothing of my country's own language! I played almost ten years in the theater — and at fifteen had no idea of the obligations of a man or citizen." In symmetrical fashion at the tale's conclusion, Karamzin reinforces that suggestion by having the Count maintain that he is typical of a great many Russians of the privileged class: "...how many of our fine countrymen try to emulate me, live without a goal, marry without love, divorce for a lark, and ruin themselves over dinners!" In this respect the hero serves as Karamzin's foil in an inverted moral allegory. By turning his audience against the hero, we can assume, Karamzin hoped to aid his readers in recognizing similar faults in themselves. Only then could they renounce their own drift towards immorality and root out their manifested shortcomings.

But there are disturbing questions unresolved in Karamzin's story when one tries to see it only as an affirmation of traditional moral and social values. For one thing there is no hint of any positive character or institution that stands against the hero. The Count is the only person who gets what he wants in this story; his program of premeditated viciousness is the only philosophy which brings any semblance of success. All the characters who trust in ordinary concepts of virtue, love, duty, etc. fail to achieve the sense of justice and personal satisfaction generally associated with those concepts. (The Count, as a self-proclaimed Lovelace, always wins; his mother's trust and love only increase her disenchantment in her son and accelerate her death; those few characters who resist the Count's depravity are the unfortunate butts of his derision and false stories.) The fact that Karamzin sought to turn his readers against the Count and his kind betrays his anxiety at their prevalence. Thus there is more than a little fear that his hero, and the class he represents, can live in defiance of the very ideals Karamzin had tried to maintain throughout his writing career.

For all the moral force Karamzin undoubtedly sought to marshal against his hero (and the social ills he entails) the disturbing vision of the Count's success is compelling. There are dark forces in life here which support the hero at each step, which protect him from the kind of retribution which figured so prominently in European and Russian fiction of the eighteenth century. Justice simply does not make itself a part of this story. The repeated vertiginous implication is that goodness does not result in happiness, but that raw cynicism and self-indulgence meet with consistent success.

The depiction in "My Confession" of life without an ethical core is the last stage of Karamzin's investigations into moral relativism. His first sketches of that unnerving concept are evident in the earlier tales in this cycle. The first crack in the monolith of his faith in sentimental optimism appeared in "Bornholm Island." The narrator's optimistic view of life was shaken by his experiences at Gravesend and on Bornholm. "Sierra Morena" enlarged those cracks for in it Karamzin represented the hostility of life to man in direct opposition to the purity of his intent (i.e., the hero's love for Elvira). In "My Confession" the crack is so enlarged that it topples the edifice of faith and a new definition of life, ruled over by moral anarchy, emerges. "My Confession" is only the culmination of Karamzin's preoccupation with the disparity between his youthful hope for universal criteria of truth and happiness (as evidenced by the *Letters* and his first cycle of tales) and life's disturbing refusal to conform to that hope (the constant factor in his second cycle).

"My Confession" is formally reminiscent of its two predecessors in its use of the travel motif. The journey is the age-old metaphor of man moving through life. His stages of travel allegorically reflect the stages of his changing world view, his evolution as a personality. The journey motif in earlier tales has already been treated in its varied forms. The sea's hostility in "Bornholm Island" alternates with the narrator's hopeful periods in which he is open to contact with other people and natural beauty. The narrator's desperate flight in "Sierra Morena," first to Palmyra's ruins and then to the north's empty coldness, clearly signals changes in his attitude away from the expectation of anything worthwhile from his life. For both narrators, the journey, like nature, parallels their degeneration of faith in life. But the Count's travels, as with so much of his activity, entail an important difference. He finds it normal to accept life without any moral foundation at all and so he does not evolve during his journies about the world; he undergoes no change of attitude. From the beginning he expects nothing worthwhile beyond the novelties of his own pleasure. The worst disappointment he ever meets is boredom. And, since there are always honest people whom he can take advantage of, that problem always finds a quick solution.

The Count's journey through Europe presents a natural juxtaposition to Karamzin's author in the *Letters.* As was pointed out in Chapter I, the travel notes bear a profound respect for beauty, knowledge, art, and the people, great and small, whom he meets along the way. All of this, of course, Count N. N. denies. His descriptions of Germany, as in the *Letters,* center on learned teachers and philosophers. But instead of immersing himself in the moral wisdom of Kant and Lavater, the Count falls asleep in his studies to save his energies for nightly revels. Instead of the balanced and objective descriptions of various religious beliefs of Europe — Catholic, Jewish, and Protestant — as presented in the *Letters,* the Count bites the Pope's foot. In the travel notes, Paris is remembered for its elegance and, especially for its lively variety in theatre. The Count, predictably, joins a band of debauchees and carouses with the notorious libertine, the Duke d'Orleans. In France, noted in the *Letters* for its modern adaptation of classical literature, the Count singles out Petronius, the author of that exposé of Roman social corruption, the *Satyricon,* as the Muse for his experiences. In England, portrayed in the notes as the land of commercial energy and an enlightened system of law, the Count straightaway drinks himself sick for a month and chases women. On his return to Russia, Count N. N., like Karamzin himself as a youth, is covered with praise and is the center of attention. Instead of the serious bearer of priceless information about Western ideas and beauty, however, the hero of "My Confession" is simply bored and uses his travels as a means of attracting female attention.

The journey in the *Letters* is, its author assures his readers, the "mirror of his soul." His is a noble and trusting soul in which faith in Enlightenment mingles with the supreme confidence that Russia can learn the lessons of that noble experiment. The journey in "My Confession" is no less a reflection of the narrator's soul and its cynicism is already obvious. The *Letters* and this tale thus represent the zenith and the nadir of Karamzin's idealism.

The thematic progression toward moral relativism is intimately linked to Karamzin's choice of narrative perspective in this group of tales. All three stories focus on a narrator, but the degree of subjectivity in each parallels exactly each narrator's increased contact with life's instability. Single *fabula* events take on meaning primarily as they help clarify his private cognition of life. In each tale of this cycle actual occurrences in the plot only take on meaning as they refer back to the organizing presence of the teller of the tale. Only those facts and occurrences which contribute to the narrator's subjective vision of life make their way into any of these three stories. The *fabula* in each is only a frame on which Karamzin arranges those distinctive opinions and feelings. In "Bornholm Island" that range was limited to the rich lyricism of sympathy and vague unspoken fears about life. In "Sierra Morena" it centers on a single passionate act of faith in life's promise of happiness (the narrator's love for Elvira) and a violent plunge into despair and anger when that promise disappears in an instant. In "My Confession" the narrow limits of the narrator's personality correspond to the aftermath of revolt — spiritual deadness and the acceptance of life as a cold vacuum.

An important distinction between the Count and his narrator-predecessors is the fact that he does not evolve. He undergoes no basic change in his world view. The others did change because of their trauma. They were willing to invest part of themselves in someone else (through sympathy or romantic love). When these worthy characters fully realized the shambles of their destroyed faith they changed, they withdrew from engagement with life. The Count, because he never hopes, is free of the trauma of betrayed faith. He lives comfortably with an untrustworthy world. His personality is strong because he wastes no energy on virtue, trust, disappointment, sadness, love, or anger. He is "free" from his own humanity, much like Stavrogin is free in Dostoevsky's *The Devils,* [11] to exert an uncanny influence on those around him.

Because *fabula* events in each story of this cycle take on meaning only in terms of the narrator's state of mind, each story can be seen as a collection of fragments. The fragments genre, pioneered by Macpherson in his Ossianic poetry, achieves the effect of recreating a sense of casual disjointedness in Karamzin's tales. In the first two tales, the fragments represent the narrator's emotional peaks and valleys of optimism and despair. [12] In "My Confession" the narrator divides his experiences into what he calls "Chinese shadows" *[kitaijskie teni].* Each reported incident from his biography attests to his private definition of life as logically disjointed and morally shapeless. The "Chinese shadows" represent the delusions most people cultivate to cover the flux and pointlessness of existence. The earlier narrators were forced to look behind some hypocritical "shadows" of justice and love. Count N. N. lives at peace with the nihilism of life in all its ramifications — not only love and justice, but education, the family, religion, duty to country, etc.

The hero-narrator of "My Confession" represents the final stage of that progression in theme and narrative method which distinguishes Karamzin's second group of tales. He gives final expression to the brewing mood of relativism which is at the seat of earlier stories in the group. Each narrator is to varying degrees cut off from the security that accompanies faith in universal truths for life.

Each narrator must of necessity view life in terms of his own isolation. These three works describe ever greater degrees of that isolation, ending with the Count's total egocentrism. This cycle of tales chronicles a growing sense of man's precarious footing over an abyss. One only has to look down, as the first two narrators by chance are forced to do, in order to see how close they are to falling. Count N. N. represents the logical conclusion to the vertigo experienced by those narrators, for he accepts an unstable existence on its own terms.

In this tale Karamzin lays to final rest his hope for putting into practice the simplified sentimental catechism of the *Letters* and his early tales. The thematic turn toward moral disorder in later tales is accompanied by Karamzin's increased emphasis on the subjective point of view in narration. Indeed, they are inseparable. As life becomes more disjointed and unreliable in the later tales, the perspective in narration correspondingly narrows until it reflects unqualified subjectivism (in the Count), a dead end in the use of the narrator. Karamzin could not create a more limited and subjective vision of life than that of the Count because the hero is the sole occupant of his world. In "My Confession" Karamzin exhausts the question of personal disillusionment just as he gives final expression to the subjective potential of the personalized narrator. His successive prose tales, almost by necessity, strike off in new directions, both in their thematics and in their narrative focus.

4

The Third Group of Tales:

Experiments with Time and Place

There is a fundamental difference between Karamzin's last works of prose fiction, considered in this chapter, and his earlier groupings of tales. In his final stories ("A Knight of Our Time," "The Sensitive and the Cold," and "Martha the Mayoress") he experiments with new definitions of his characters, their inner psychological potential, and the way they relate to their social environment. The tendency of each work's subject matter is to explore the psychic development of individuals within the specifics of their time and place.

In both the earlier cycles, Karamzin defined his *personae* in a basically asocial sense. The first group of tales approached characters most often as examples of one or another sentimental ideals (e.g., filial piety, personal virtue, the power of romantic love, etc.). Natalia, Liza, or the dwarf in "The Beautiful Princess" drew their identify directly from those abstract principles. They made decisions and lived by their results primarily in schematized responses to the prompting of their hearts rather than to believable mores of their class or time in history. In these early pieces Karamzin subscribed to that brand of sentimentalism (represented in the novels of Richardson, Rousseau, and in certain Masonic ideals) which stressed the innate right of the individual to leap the strictures of his society and live in an idealized democracy of spiritual equality. That is to say, Karamzin's early characters exemplify the high aspirations of the sentimental alternative to material and social reality. Indeed, it is that stage in Karamzin's writing career which has encouraged Soviet critics like L. I. Timofeev to criticize his attempt to "depict reality as he [Karamzin] wanted to see it, . . . to depict it in accordance with the scheme to which it [reality] must be subordinate."[1] Timofeev is correct in saying that Karamzin in his early brand of sentimentalism "sought to draw characters within the scope of uni-dimensional psychology and was attracted to themes which were devoid of social coloration."[2] In balancing Timofeev's prejudice against sentimental ideology in those early tales, however, it is only fair to say that the sacrifice of objective social reality in favor of depicting the transcendent ideals of virtue and feeling was what Karamzin hoped to accomplish.

Society as a bundle of externally tangible facts, mores, and values, was not an integral part of the intended design. Erast in "Poor Liza" is partially rounded because he loves Liza, yet he rejects her in favor of a rich widow of his own class. But that social problem is subordinated to the sentimental emphasis on a peasant girl who is capable of the same kind of love as a well-bred Moscow lady ("even peasants know how to love!"). Julia is capable of a good deal of inner complexity as she wavers between the quiet contentment of her family and the gaudy appeal of

Count N. But her decision is fundamentally made in terms of the dilemma of "natural morality" *à la* Rousseau rather than any developed social expectation or pressure which her milieu exerts on her.

Karamzin's second group of tales is also essentially asocial in scope, treating characters in various stages of romantic withdrawal from social interaction. In each of these stories the character-narrator assumes identify through his private, internalized interpretation of life. He stands outside social intercourse, fully immersed in the fluctuations of his own emotional condition. Reality for him is a relative thing, dependent on his own state of mind at the moment as he gives free rein to his introspective tendencies. The natural result, as with romanticism as a movement, is that the character is "filled" by his own strong emotions to such an extent that he "overflows" (as Wordsworth put it), imparting to his physical and social surroundings exactly those qualities he senses so poignantly in himself (hence the exotic and isolated locales Karamzin chooses for these tales). Thus, based on his experiences at Gravesend and on Bornholm the narrator of "Bornholm Island" muses aloud about the general instability of progress. The narrator of "Sierra Morena" is stronger in his renunciation of life and society because his personal experiences are more traumatic. Count N. N. in "My Confession" carries such relativism to its furthest point as he, almost from birth, projects the ethical vacuum of his own soul onto all of existence, entertaining no possible standards which differ from his own. His is the strongest expression of the individual who lives in a world of his own making. For him, social values are so many "Chinese shadows;" rules are "halters for weak minds" to which ordinary people dumbly conform.

Karamzin's youthful and exuberant faith in life

within the framework of sentimental ideals, then, tends to fragment into a rudderless sense of individual relativism in his tales written from the mid 1790's to 1802. As was mentioned earlier, the atmosphere of gloom and decay in the second cycle of tales corresponds to Karamzin's own sense of estrangement in those years. On the basis of Karamzin's biography and correspondence, it is most probable that his personal pessimism intensified in the late 1790s, because of the repressive reign of Tsar Paul [3] and the failure of the French Revolution (as Makogonenko suggests). The author was virtually in exile from Moscow, its social questions and its intelligentsia. The precariousness of his position is evidenced, for example, by his near arrest on trumped-up charges of anti-Tsarist writings.

With the ascension of Alexander I in 1801, Karamzin underwent a personal renaissance of confidence in an ordered monarchy within which humanistic goals, aided by enlightened laws, could allow the growth of the individual's fullest potential. He raises the stability of that fair society above the personality of any individual citizen. In his critique of alternative social experiments, such as republicanism, Karamzin writes: "My heart, no less than others, is stirred by the virtue of the great republicans; but how short-lived are their brilliant epochs. How often in the name of freedom was tyranny used . . . " [4] Moreover, the monarch, as the legitimate head of that ordered society, is equally subject to its common weal. In his remarks about Catherine II in his "Historical Panagyric to Catherine II" ["Istoričeskoe poxval'noe slovo Ekaterine II"], Karamzin especially extols what he terms (albeit myopically) her principle that "subjects do not exist for the monarchs, but monarchs [exist] for their subjects."

Karamzin's faith in monarchist order as the best hope for personal fulfillment represents a tangibly social basis for his vision of enlightenment as opposed to the more abstractly spiritual or sentimental idealism of his early prose. His new emphasis is very much on the palpable level of *this* life, fixed in time and place, within a distinct historical continuum. Karamzin's initiation of the *Messenger of Europe* in 1802 bears ample testimony to his creation of a prestigious national forum in which Russians could discuss European and domestic political, cultural, and literary events. His growing attention to Russia's independent identity in each of these areas takes the form of active patriotism. As he remarks: "There is a limit and a measure to all things: as with an individual so it is with a nation. It necessarily begins with emulation but it must eventually exist in and of itself." [5]

Karamzin's exhortation to his country to "stand boldly alongside other [nations], pronouncing its own name bravely, repeating it with noble pride" [6] was not a mere exercise in chauvinism, but the practical understanding of two related needs for Russia: first, it must assume its rightful role as a viable socio-historical entity; second, its individual citizens must define themselves within that national entity to a significant degree. With the ascension of Alexander to the throne, Karamzin's optimism about posing such questions reveals itself in his renewed interest in journalism, social philosophy, and his growing fascination with Russian history.

In his late fiction Karamzin consistently formulates the same basic question in personal terms of his characters (i.e., what are the limits of an individual's uniqueness of character relative to the larger context of influences in which he develops.) In the late tales he assesses, from a number of different vantage points, the relations between personal (psychological) distinctiveness in his *personae* and the values of their time and place. For the first time

Karamzin coordinates the psychological viability of characters with the tangible limits of their social milieu. It is that dual emphasis which unites these last tales and makes them distinctive as a body from preceding works.

The specifics of that link between society and the psychological uniqueness of central characters vary among the three works considered here, for Karamzin speculates freely on different approaches to that essential question. In "A Knight of Our Time" he develops a Lockean thesis that each individual is the sum total of the experiences his environment holds for him. In "The Sensitive and the Cold" he poses the reverse, maintaining that different potentials or tendencies distinguish each person from his birth. One's innate psychological propensities reveal themselves at each stage of personal growth, organizing external stimuli into a pattern of cognition and behavior fundamentally consistent with one's unchangeable "nature." In "Martha the Mayoress" Karamzin chooses a radically different modus to investigate the complex interplay between external environment and the inner mechanism of an individual's personality. In this, the first Russian historical tale worthy of the name, Karamzin raises the individuality of his major characters (especially Martha) to a heroic level, integrating their personalities into the larger socio-historical issues of their time. As characters resolve those large issues, as they act out their private sense of duty, they are defined as individuals.

As is the case throughout Karamzin's career as a prose writer, the angle(s) of vision he chooses within the narrative process relates directly to his handling of *fabula*. An examination of narrative point of view in these last tales helps clarify his overall compositional design. As will be discussed in more detail later, Karamzin adopts a combination of narrative modes consisting of neutral omniscience, which is more extensively present in these tales than in the past, and editoral omniscience, a mode used extensively in his earliest prose.

Neutral omniscience is a major component of the historical development of realism, with its metonymic, descriptive emphasis. Karamzin's attention to those empirical tools within the narrative task suggests his experimentation with principles of realism long before it was to gather momentum in Russia. Through his use of editorial omniscience (especially in "A Knight of Our Time" and in "The Sensitive and the Cold") Karamzin conveys periodic judgment about a work's meaning directly to the reader, much as he did in his earliest prose. This point of view provides a superior vantage point in the tales which Karamzin integrates into the metonymic texture of netural omniscience. Both narrative modes combine to emphasize the central issue of personality formation within a recognizable social environment. To put it in Booth's terms, one point of view "shows" while the other "tells" or explains what transpires in the work. "Martha," with its distinctively heroic structure, relies on both the objectivity of descriptions and the sort of editorial comment common to the epic poet. In addition, again in compliance with heroic traditions, Karamzin utilizes the formal monolog of his characters as a complement to his other narrative modes.

"A KNIGHT OF OUR TIME"

"Rycar' našego vremeni" ["A Knight of Our Time"] [7] (1802-1803) has no unified plot in the ordinary sense. It follows the developing psychological and physical capacities of a Russian child (Leon) of the late eighteenth-century rustic gentry. The tale describes his growth until the age of eleven, interweaving the successive sets of stimuli which act on him with his own expanding cognition. Compositionally, the tale consists of thirteen short chapters, each of which is built around a group of related experiences or impressions. Logically enough there is a gradual increase in complexity in those stimuli together with the hero's correspondingly greater capacities to absorb them. Chapter I gives a summary of the locale in which Leon's parents lived before his birth, "the cultivated side of the Volga where it joins with the clear Sviyaga River." Chapter II describes his physical attributes at birth; Chapter III depicts his "natural" early education which is modeled after that of Rosseau's Émile (e.g., his mother nursed him herself, took an active role in teaching him to talk and walk, expressed her feelings openly to the child, and encouraged the same from him). Chapter IV is given over to authorial comment on the unpredictability of events which occur in each individual's life. It is the only non-descriptive chapter in the tale. The unhappy death of Leon's mother and its melancholy effects on him (examples of that unpredictability) figure prominently in Chapter V. In Chapter VI the hero's first exposure to literature and its enormous influence on his imagination are most salient. His early religious experiences appear in Chapter VII and Chapter VIII develops around a description of the adult males who exert an influence on him by the example of their life style (a mixture of rowdy, naive fun and the most serious devotion to honor, loyalty and brotherly love).

Chapter IX introduces the first glimmer of Leon's internal imagination as founded on his exposure to a wider range of reading. His first experiences with books (Chapter VI) present Leon as a "Columbus" who sails the world of the printed word as the earlier explorer had navigated the

Atlantic. Leon's reading habits in Chapter IX center on romances in which he identifies with the adventurous heroes. His growing powers of conceptualization take the form here of projecting fantasies of himself onto the fictional situations of his stories. His developing imagination prepares him for the important events of Chapter X which describe Leon's chance acquaintance with a rich neighbor whose wife (Emilia) stirs Leon's memories of his own mother, both in her physical appearance and in her tender personality. Chapter XI is a digression in that it veers away from primary concern with Leon in order to describe his mother-surrogate's biography. The purpose, as it relates to the overall composition of the story, is to explain the cause for Emilia's warm response to Leon in his need for maternal love. Married to an older and unfeeling man, she is nevertheless in need of a focus for her own emotional warmth. Discarding the alternative of taking a lover, she directs her love toward Leon, thereby providing her contribution to the symbiotic relationship which develops between them.

Chapter XII traces the growth of Leon's attachment to his new mother as she teaches him the ways of the world. Her influence is important because it comes at a time when Leon starts to grow out of childhood. With Emilia's help he learns how to dress *à la mode,* and discovers the charms of music. These stimuli, clustered around the presence of a beautiful woman, lead Leon to the first stirrings of sexual awareness. The last chapter serves as an illustration of that maturing sexuality. Fascinated by his "mother's" private moments, he seeks out the place where she bathes and then frequents the spot. On one occasion he is surprised by her appearance but stays hidden to watch her undress. His faster pulse is only vaguely tied to any sexual awareness (he is eleven at the time) but he is obviously moving quickly into adolescence. Leon is discovered and he suffers his first deep humiliation. Emilia is more than ready to forgive him, however, and the close bond between them continues unbroken if not strengthened. Karamzin breaks off his narrative at this point and one can only speculate about what he had planned for his "Christopher Columbus" as he was to explore the mysteries of his changing self and an increasingly complex world.

The composition of "A Knight" articulates on Locke's thesis of the *tabula rasa,* that an individual's personality development is determined by those influences which his environment happens to transmit to him. In Chapter II, Karamzin editorially asserts that the individual's personality, values, and manner of cognition represent the total of those stimuli. He emphasizes Locke's idea that the newborn infant is a "blank piece of paper" on which his experiences leave indelible traces. Single stimuli (like those described in Leon's attachment to his mother, his religious experiences, and the adult males who teach him the meaning of loyalty) soon merge into more complex patterns. These, in turn, help him determine the meaning of new experiences, translating them into the context of what he has already learned. As Ernest Tuveson says of the Lockean theory of knowledge, the mind "has the power to arrange the simple ideas, the impressions, in patterns that enable the animal man to cope with his environment." [8] As these single experiences become more numerous (as they gradually do for Leon) they tend to reinforce one another, triggering associations of varying complexity (e.g., Leon's perceived similarity between Emilia and his mother as he remembers her).

The thesis of empirical cognition and personality formation is worked out carefully in Karamzin's arrangement of the tale's composition into chapters, each of which represents related incidents and stimuli which contribute to the general direction of the hero's personal maturation. Karamzin works on two irreducible levels of composition in this story to give formal expression to that central idea. On one level he theorizes on the Lockean concept of how people develop as personalities. The second level is more tangible, for here Karamzin enumerates those specific instances of influence and experience. He recounts numerous situations which flesh out the theory of psychological determinism, portraying with great delicacy the dynamic formation of a rounded personality from the "blank paper" of infancy.

As in Karamzin's earlier works, his choice of narrative points of view in "A Knight" is integral to the subject matter and compositional structure. In this important respect he is both innovative and revives older narrative angles to carry out his experiment with the *Bildungsroman*. By way of innovation he develops the potential of neutral omniscience (third person narration) to a much greater degree than in any of his preceding tales. Through this mode he emphasizes the accumulation of specific facts, free of editorial asides, about Leon's life at each stage of his maturation. These gradually form a stable channel through which information about his surroundings and experiences flows steadily to the reader. As is typical of the mode historically, it focuses on metonymic details which, as Dmitrij Čiževskij points out, "lead from the presented object to its environment." [9]

Such objective facts form a firm base of information pertinent to different stages of the hero's growth. They bear no overt opinion but stand as individual facts which "speak for themselves." They are primarily descriptive, not interpretive. For example in Chapter III ("His Early

Childhood"), where Leon's mother figures prominently as his "natural" teacher, we read: "Already external objects began to excite his attention; already with his eyes, the movement of his hand, and his words he often asked his mother: 'What do I see? What do I hear?' Already he was learning how to walk and run; but nothing absorbed him as much as his mother's caresses. . ." Chapter VI ("Successes in Study and the Formation of His Mind and Feelings") is devoted to the hero's early exposure to fiction and the impression it makes on his malleable values: "He had an unusually good understanding [of reading] and after a few months he could read all the religious books like *Our Father* and he quickly acquired the ability to write. He also learned as quickly to read secular writing, to the astonishment of the neighboring landowners. His father regularly had Leon read in their presence to enjoy their praises in his own heart." In Chapter X ("An Important Acquaintance") Leon makes the important symbolic association between Countess Mirova (Emilia) and his deceased mother. That scene is presented through neutral omniscience: "The appearance of the Count (a man of about fifty) further magnified his timidity. But, looking at the pretty Countess, Leon gathered his courage. He continued to stare at her and suddenly his face changed. He started to cry, wanted to hide his tears and could not."

Pertinent information about his growing mental agility often appears matter-of-factly as in the following passage: "His successes with French were even more surprising. Having had no experience with dull grammar, in three months he could already express in that language his thankful love to his mama [Emilia] and he knew perfectly all the subtleties of affectionate expressions." In Chapter XIII neutral omniscience figures prominently in the presentation of Leon's increasingly complex relationships with others. His attitude toward Emilia as a mother surrogate necessarily expands to that of a woman when he unwittingly observes her at her bath. As happens throughout the tale, his old conceptions constantly admit new shades of meaning, given the stimuli of novel situations and events: "He fell exhausted to the ground and breathed with difficulty. After an hour he returned for his clothing with a dejected countenance, but, when he saw that a rose had been pinned to his hat, his spirits returned. 'Mama isn't angry with me!,' he thought. He dressed and went to her. . . However, he blushed when he looked at Emilia; she wanted to smile and also blushed."

Stylistically, these sections of neutral omniscience emphasize a broad spectrum of tangible, metonymic facts which are free of any direct authorial intrusions, explanations, or deductions. As the story progresses chronologically, more empirical evidence accumulates as the reader perceives on his own the distinct stages of the hero's physical and psychological growth. Each of those stages, conveniently divided into chapters, is based on a variety of controlled disruptions of Leon's earlier world view. He successfully incorporates these regular disruptions into an increasingly complex cognition of himself and of his world. Karamzin thereby establishes a fundamental sense of reader involvement in the hero's evolution, not through the intermediate personality of a narrator, as in earlier tales, but by the sheer accumulation of fact and detail. As a result, neutral omniscience plays a significant compositional role in the implicit dynamic of the *Bildundsroman.*

Together with his experiments with the use of neutral omniscience, Karamzin revitalizes the intruding author device (editorial omniscience) to order and explain the extensive network of facts introduced piecemeal through the neutral omniscience mode. The commenting author is no longer a moral presence, as he was in earlier tales. Rather, Karamzin uses the device in this tale to summarize and explain directly the progress of Leon's maturation at each stage. In his guise as commenting author, Karamzin periodically pauses long enough to consolidate masses of seemingly random detail which accumulate in passages of neutral omniscience. Utilizing the mode's characteristic properties of digression, generalization and humor, Karamzin works authorial commentary into a coherent pattern which imposes an external order on the numerous stimuli and experience which stimulate Leon's growth. The author's pattern of intrusion is thus correlative with the metonymic pattern of neutral omniscience.

It is as Karamzin's spokesman for the Lockean thesis that the intruding author can best be understood and his numerous appearances in the work integrated. Speaking through the auctorial privilege, Karamzin says: "Nature casts us into the world as into a dark, dense forest, without any ideas or information, but with a large reservoir of curiosity which begins to function early in the infant, all the earlier as the *basis* of his soul is tender and perfect. This is the white cloud at the dawn of life from behind which rises the sun of knowledge and experience!" He goes on to contrast the impact of ten weeks of a child's earliest experiences with the later, intellectual effect of ideas and information acquired by a mature adult in ten years, generalizing "the scales tip unquestionably to the former." Earlier he draws attention to the pristine quality of a child before experiences mold his mind and emotions into distinctive patterns: "Let us call infancy a beautiful pool on which it is well and good to look and praise in a few words, but which I do not recommend for a poet's lengthy description." The reason for this, he goes on to say, is that nothing is happening on the calm surface of that psychic pool. One can praise its innocence, but any more attention "will only make one yawn and fall asleep" because of its vacancy. Only after the turbulance of experience can the pool, to continue his analogy, attract curiosity and interest. It is the voice of the intruding author that Karamzin chooses to crystallize the work's thesis ("the soul of a newborn infant is a blank piece of paper") and connect it with Locke's name.

Karamzin freely uses the intruding author device to highlight several related aspects of the Lockean thesis. These include, first, the idea that the earliest experiences are the most important and to a large extent determine how the individual will interpret later events and relationships. Second, the intruding author fixes firmly for his readers the limits of cognition which correspond to the individual's own level of maturity. As commentator, Karamzin draws a clear distinction between how his child-hero perceives a situation as opposed to the way an adult would interpret it. Third, Karamzin authorially draws on Lockean psychology to establish the principle of randomness in what occurs in life and how it influences the maturing mind of the individual. Each of these correlative aspects of Lockean thought is worked out by example in neutral omniscience. But, by presenting them as general principles through the voice of the intruding author, Karamzin greatly enhances their clarity.

In Chapter VI, Karamzin describes the details of Leon's early exposure to reading, much of which has a moral tone — virtue is rewarded, vice is punished. Assuming an auctorial pose, Karamzin emphasizes the importance of that exposure in forming Leon's character and how it will continue to influence him throughout life: "Ach! Leon in his mature years will often see the repulsive, but his heart will not part from its comforting system. Against all adversity it will say: 'No, no! The victory of sin is an illusion, an apparition!' " In the next chapter, which describes the young hero's religious experiences, Karamzin intervenes in the narration briefly to emphasize the importance of early influences on his hero's later values: "Leon will never be an atheist, even if he reads Spinoza and Hobbes' *System of Nature.*"

The author varies the kind of early influences which help form Leon's character, but he never veers from his emphasis on their long-lasting effects on the hero. He makes a point of saying those influences will remain in him for life: "In his childhood Leon listened with pleasure to your [the influential males of his childhood] garrulous conversations. From you he learned Russian friendliness, from you he obtained that Russian spirit and noble pride of the gentry which later he was not to find even in famous boyars." Hypothesizing that early reading accelerates and directs the individual's spiritual growth, Karamzin opines: "I confess that we can call them [novels] a hothouse for the young soul which, because of this reading, ripens faster than usual." Venturing further into his digression, he takes to task those numerous "phlegmatics" and "egoists" who inveigh against reading as at best a waste of time and, at its worst, downright harmful. [10] Karamzin-as-author is careful to point out that Leon, because of the leavening effect of literature, will be saved from becoming like those stultified and limited critics: "My hero takes off his cap and bows low to you and says with all respect: 'Dear Sirs! You will never see me under your banners.' " After Leon's mother is dead, he grieves over her absence and senses keenly the need to continue the loving relationship she had provided. It is only natural, says the author, for him to seek its renewal with a mother substitute, thereby restating the dictum that early stimuli affect future expectation and choice: "Ach! the best parent can never replace the mother, the most tender being on earth! Only a woman's love, ever attentive and tender, satisfies the heart in all its relations!. . . Thus was Leon prepared by nature, fate and novels for what followed." What follows is Leon's projection of those desires for maternal love on Emilia, who bears a strong physical resemblance to his mother.

As intruding author, Karamzin is careful to structure Leon's psychological development within the limits of a child's cognition. When he describes his young hero's close physical contact with the beautiful Emilia, he is careful to point out the hero's natural innocence: "Lucky child! If you were eight years older [he is eleven at this point] — who would not envy your good fortune. But you are beholden to your very youth for your rare good fortune!" Continuing to emphasize the limitations of sexual knowledge in Leon, Karamzin digresses on the subject: "The reader will think . . . that we are preparing him for something objectionable to [Leon's] innocence: No! . . that time still lies ahead! Our hero is just barely eleven years old. . ." Drawing attention to Leon's sexual limits through his use of humor, Karamzin clearly distinguishes between what the boy sees as Emilia prepares for her bath and what mature adults would see: "We oldsters know everything; we know what is possible to see and that we must keep quiet about it. On the other hand, need one describe in a novel such things as (thanks to the style of the time!) what everyone can see at parties, balls and taking a walk? . . . I must look at things strictly through the eyes of my hero — and he did not see anything! . . ."

The Lockean theory of developmental psychology advances the idea of randomness in what stimuli will leave their marks on the "blank page" of youthful minds and emotions. It is that random pattern of influence which progressively prepares the individual to assimilate the complexity of experience, to mature. The clearest positing of that principle of randomness in experience takes place in Chapter IV: *"This is exactly what happened! . . . —* and I shall not say a word more. Is it appropriate? Is it proper? None of that is my affair. I simply trail after fate pen in hand and describe what it does according to its own omnipotent design. If you wonder why, then ask it, but I will tell you in advance that you will receive no answer." He spends the rest of this chapter (it is only one paragraph in length) discoursing on the unpredictability of events and their haphazardness (e.g., evil people seem to live forever while the best seem to die in their youth; "the rose withers while the thorn remains;" the grand oak is felled by lightning while the upas-tree is untouched, etc.). The principle of randomness in Leon's case is attested to in the next chapter in which his mother dies suddenly, before her time. The unexpected blow, of course, touches off a chain reaction of events which eventually lead the hero into a close attachment with Emilia, who in turn is responsible for influencing Leon's education, his sensibilities, his sexual awareness, etc.

As in some of his early tales, Karamzin uses editorial humor in "A Knight" to emphasize what he says in the guise of intruding author. For example, in his introduction to the tale Karamzin-as-author makes a point of spoofing the gothic or tendentious historical fiction then popular. He calls that type of prose, along with its resurrected wise and ancient heroes, an "excellent puppet show" which reduces the reader to yawning. He prefers instead an ordinary person from the near past as the hero of his story, emphasizing that sort's greater claim to believability. He ends his humorous positing of an inherently serious criterion in character selection with the folk aphorism: "If you don't like don't listen, but don't bother me while I tell it" *[Ne ljubo ne slušaj, a govorit' ne mešaj].* In his amusing restatement of an old country woman's predictions about Leon's future at his birth, Karamzin auctorially emphasizes the varied life awaiting his hero. She sees "happiness and misfortune for him, fine weather and storms, riches and poverty, friends and enemies, success in love and occasional horns." The author then wittily responds: "The reader will see that the wise old woman did indeed have the gift of prophesy." Beneath his banter Karamzin is making the same point as in other, more serious digressions, that randomness of experience leads to a rounded personality in real people (as opposed to the "puppets" of historical adventures). The comic use of the commenting author is most certainly inspired here by Sterne as it was in earlier tales like "Natalia" or "The Beautiful Princess." But its structural function within the narrative, as in those early pieces, is carefully subordinated to a larger and more serious compositional design.

"A Knight" represents a new direction for Karamzin's concept of character as both unidealized and reliant on environment for his personality and his system of values. Its narrative scheme is very much a part of that experimentation. Reworking the older narrative device of the intruding author, he removes it from its earlier role of preaching general rules of moral conduct and sentimental ideals. Karamzin uses it instead to organize and make clear the more objective question of how social milieu influences a new member in a variety of ways. Neutral omniscience, on the other hand, assumes a prominence which it never had in Karamzin's earlier tales. By that mode he establishes the empirical base on which the central principle of social influence is erected. Through his eclecticism in narrative technique, Karamzin provides an early example of those metonymic links between material environment and a character's mental processes which later figure so prominently in the Russian novel.

"THE SENSITIVE AND THE COLD"

"Čuvstvitel'nyj i xolodnyj" ["The Sensitive and the Cold"] [11] (1803) continues Karamzin's examination of how the individual personality develops and how it relates to its social environment. He expands his interest here, however, to treat different personality types, as well as to trace their experiences throughout their lives, even to the point of recounting their respective deaths. In this story the thesis is that the limits of one's personality are fixed at birth; various experiences do not change the personality so much as reveal its potential as one moves through life. That assumption, which is clearly proposed at the tale's outset, puts the work squarely opposite the *tabula rasa* statement so apparent in "A Knight," published but a few months earlier.

There is no unified plot line in this tale, a quality it shares with its immediate predecessor. Karamzin composes the tale out of a series of contrasts which regularly place his heroes in the same situation vis-à-vis their common society. Within each new set of circumstances Erast (the "sensitive," emotional man) and Leonid (the "cold," calculating man) exemplify their unalterable limits of behavior. [12] The result is a thorough representation of human nature as fixed at birth. For example, as youths attending the same school, they already present clearly opposite qualities: "In [Erast] there appeared from his earliest years a rare sensitivity: [Leonid], it seemed, was born prudent." Erast learns quickly but rarely retains anything from his studies while Leonid acquires information slowly but forgets nothing. Erast, as an imaginative child, loves literature and gives himself over to imagination while Leonid prefers the more enduring facts of history. Confronted with the need to decide quickly, as they are when their *pension* suddenly burns, Erast saves some of his professor's valuables and leaves his own belongings behind. Leonid, unrattled by the emergency, saves both his and Erast's necessary clothing and books, chiding his friend for his imprudence.

Both enter the army at the same time. Erast, burning with impatience to gain glory and save the homeland, is almost immediately captured. Leonid, circumspect as always, contents himself with carrying out his orders punctually and with precision. They start simultaneous careers in the civil service only to have them result in a manner consistent with each's essential nature. Erast quarrels with his superior when he differs with the latter's opinions and soon is forced to leave his government post. Leonid performs each task with tact and care. Turning his lack of imagination into a bureaucratic virtue he rises steadily into positions of ever-increasing authority. As Erast moves erratically from one love entanglement to another, Leonid avoids any serious contact with women until he feels the need for the kind of order in his domestic affairs which might correspond to his regular office routine. As he explains it to Erast: "I shall marry in a month in order to excuse myself from household concerns. A woman is necessary for a home's proper regimen."

At times Karamzin's interest in setting up the contrastive responses of his heroes within the same social situation lapses into the schematic. When Leonid as a bachelor visits Erast and his bride, she falls in love with the assured, aloof stranger. Rather than let any unpleasantness result from his presence, Leonid simply leaves. When Erast (after his divorce) visits Leonid and his new wife, he falls in love with the new mistress of the house. Even though he wishes to leave, he cannot master the demands of his strong emotions and he remains. Leonid has to solve the problem by moving away, taking his wife with him.

With the passage of time, each character achieves the kind of fame which most fits his respective nature. Erast's undisciplined and spontaneous emotions lead him to write poetry and his success is meteoric. However, impulsiveness is not only the key to his fortune, it is his reason for abandoning literature as well. His impossible love for Leonid's wife brings with it a paralyzing melancholy as he forsakes all attempts at communication, preferring to wander in his grief. Leonid, on the other hand, achieves respect and a high rank in the government thanks to his clarity of thought and his ability to carry out a given task without asking unnecessary questions. His successes are as firmly rooted in his lack of imagination as Erast's are in his superabundance of that quality.

Karamzin presents each character's death in a manner fully in keeping with his irreducible personality. Erast, worn out physically and spiritually by his tempestuous life, dies still trying to harmonize his unfulfilled desires with resisting fate. Leonid finishes his life as he had innumerable reports — efficiently and with no expenditure of fortuitous energy ("He died with no desires or fear, just as he usually fell asleep at night.").

The openness with which Karamzin formulates his tale's thesis, that human nature is inborn and unalterable, makes its subject matter unavoidably contrastive with "A Knight." Erast and Leonid emerge as rounded characters as they evolve on their parallel migrations from the cradle to the grave. Unlike Leon, however, these characters unfold rather than change. Each set of social stimuli they meet expands the reader's familiarity with them, but always in keeping with the strict limits suggested by the key words of the story's title — "sensitive" and "cold." The specifics of their social milieu are important as they provide a believable range of choices within which each character's innate bent finds expression. Indeed, the clarity of Karamzin's vision of inborn personality has led some critics to question the work's consideration as *belles lettres* at all. Makogonenko has the opinion that "it is not a tale, a short story, or a sketch in its genre. Most probably it should be termed a psychological étude." [13] Makogonenko's perplexity is understandable. Although Karamzin develops a sense of depth in each character's personality, they are so neatly contrastive that they lend themselves to the symmetrical function of a philosopher's example as much as to autonomous literary constructs. By their representation of polar types, meeting the same situations but always making decisions consistent with their essential natures, Karamzin argues the credence of man's preformed personality (hence Makogonenko's suggestion of the "psychological étude").

Leaving aside the question of its proper genre designation, it is perhaps more profitable to examine how Karamzin achieves the effects that constitute "The Sensitive and the Cold." The seeming dichotomy between short story and philosophical tract here derives largely from Karamzin's choice of narrative technique. Much of the tale is devoted to numerous detailed descriptions of the heroes' contrastive behavior. These sections appear in neutral omniscience. There results a gradual sense of familiarity with Erast and Leonid as personae. That familiarity brings with it the illusion of objectivity and verisimilitude as the reader follows the development of the heroes' intellectual and emotional potentials throughout their lives. At the same time, Karamzin continues his reliance on editorial omniscience to clarify the issue of inborn limits. In this respect Leonid and Erast serve as examples of a principle greater than themselves (hence their schematic quality).

Karamzin relies more on neutral omniscience in this tale than in any earlier one. The mode's increased presence provides more of an emphasis on the "minute recital of common-place events" through which the reader forms his perception of each hero's manner of decision making and behavior. When in their youth they see a child drowning, Karamzin displays their opposite actions and behavior in neutral omniscience: "Erast let out a cry and threw himself into the water. Leonid tried to restrain him but was not in time. However, he did not lose his head, nor did he even cry out, but set out running as fast as he could toward fishermen who were straightening out their nets in the distance. He threw them a ruble and had them save Erast who was already drowning." The narrative tone here is one of disinterested transcription of facts as they occur.

Karamzin is no less intent on "letting facts speak for themselves" when he ventures into drawing the inner states of mind characteristic of his heroes. After his marriage, Erast experiences a reduction in his ardor for life, as if he had reached the peak of happiness and had only the downward slope to contemplate: "He relished his love and peace alike, but soon he noticed in himself a surprising predisposition to melancholy. He often fell into thought, was dejected, and was glad when he had a chance to weep." Leonid's psyche is more orderly than Erast's and is given to a narrow range of aspirations, fears, hopes and motives: "He did a great deal of good, but without any kind of inner pleasure, but only for his own safety. He did not respect people but was wary of them; he did not seek pleasure, but avoided disappointment. Nonsuffering seemed to him enjoyment, and equanimity — the talisman of wisdom."

Karamzin's designation of more space to neutral omniscience and its empirical emphasis continues a tendency already apparent in "A Knight." As well, his use of the intruding author to place the resulting accumulation of facts into manageable perspective repeats his use of that narrative mode in "A Knight." It should be emphasized that Karamzin avoids the tags of "right" or "wrong," "good" or "bad" when he assumes the authorial stance in his late fiction. Rather, he uses the mode to expand on the contrastive qualities and traits of human types represented by the heroes. Karamzin turns the commenting author from arguing for sentimental ideals to emphasizing the tale's thesis of personality formation. Karamzin, as intruding author, is most direct in formulating the work's thesis at the very outset: "Nature alone creates and endows [the personality]. Rearing only gives it form . . . Like a person's mind, his character is its concern. A father, a teacher, conditions, can aid his ultimate development, but nothing more." He supports his theory with the authority of La Fontaine's dictum: "We are eternally what we are fated to be. Drive nature out the door — it will fly in through the window," to make his thesis more vivid. Numerous authorial intrusions in the tale proper serve to support that assertion. For example, he says of Erast (and his "category" of passionate people): "Tender hearts are always ready to forgive nobly and they rejoice at the idea that they acquire in the process new claims on the love of the guilty one . . . " Erast's behavior, motives, and manner of cognition often serve the intruding author to make general observations on this type: "The reader can forgive Erast [he had just come close to starting an affair with Leonid's wife]: the gnawing of his conscience has already punished him. For the tender heart, no possible calamity can compare with those instances when he must reproach himself." Most of these parenthetical observations pertain to Erast — as a type his experiences and motives range as far as the variety of his moods and passing causes. The phlegmatic Leonid, on the other hand, receives less editorial attention in the way of reference to a general category of man. For example, in discussing his aloof attitude toward women, Karamzin interjects the generalization: "Speaking of that, we have noticed that cold people sometimes appeal to women more than the sensitive. The latter reveal themselves too hastily and without any *economy*. The first hide behind the shield of equanimity and arouse curiosity which works strongly on a woman's imagination."

Karamzin is careful to use his auctorial prerogative to describe the essential personality of each hero, its strong and weak qualities alike. He refuses to sit in judgment on them. In assessing sensitive people in general he points out they are keenly aware of the compulsions in their nature: "Truly, the sensitive alone know this compulsion. The cold are always satisfied with themselves and do not desire to change. Does this observation alone prove that advantage and happiness fall to them [the cold]?" He then compensates for his opinion by continuing: "The sensitive undoubtedly enjoy themselves more; but since there is more unhappiness than pleasure in life, it is an advantage to feel both to a lesser extent [as do the cold]." While contending openly that sensitive types are noble in their draining the cup of experience, Karamzin editorially balances the scales by immediately pointing out the justifiable superiority enjoyed by the phlegmatic person: "On the other hand, for the sake of justice, we note his advantages. Indifferent people are more judicious in all matters, they live quieter in society, cause less unhappiness and less often disturb social harmony . . . "

The use of editorial omniscience, then, is approached in such a way as to complement the descriptive quality of neutral omniscience. The central juxtaposition of different personality categories on the basis of cognition and behavior shows through clearly in both narrative modes and emerges as the unifying compositional design. Metonymic examples alternate with declarative exposition on what is implied by those examples. "The Sensitive and the Cold" thus continues to pose the basic question so visible in "A Knight" — "how and why does an individual develop psychologocally as he does?" The main distinction between the two works is that of what answer Karamzin gives to his question. With only slight modification, his experimental narrative technique serves either answer.

"MARTHA THE MAYORESS"

In "Marfa-posadnica ili pokorenie Novagoroda" ["Martha the Mayoress or the Subdual of Novgorod"] [14] (1803), Karamzin continues his interest in the related questions of new visions of character definition and a developed social context, but with some important changes. Chief among these is the fact that he chooses a historical theme and setting containing a momentous event in Russian national history — the fifteenth-century conflict between republican Novgorod and Moscow's growing hegemony as the seat of monarchist rule. Karamzin approaches that conflict not only with the vigor of a poet, but also as a historian absorbed in depicting his country's evolution as an autonomous state. His interests here are, first, to give an accurate account of the actual background from which that conflict arose and, second, to recreate in his main characters a sense of elevated importance associated with the key arbiters of that conflict. Consequently Karamzin approaches society with specific historical limits (i.e., in its period detail, its problems, and the options for action open to its important figures). Characters here draw their identity directly from their historical context and are subordinate to its outcome for their meaning and interest.

Karamzin's literary ordering of historic social issues in "Martha" is accomplished by a number of long-standing epic conventions. These conventions go back both to Homer and, more recently, to eighteenth-century versions of national *poemas.* In the same spirit Karamzin chose the elevated narrative point of view common to the epic to convey his story. Epic *topoi,* including the heroic perspective of its telling, govern the reader's response to the historical issues Karamzin raises. More specifically the work's epic design provides Karamzin with a much-respected model for examining the complex interplay between questions of personal will and social limits of time and place. Such questions were central to both "A Knight of Our Time" and "The Sensitive and the Cold," but in more abstract form. The epic elements in "Martha" provide the means for making specific those questions within a distinctively national context.

The connection of art to important moments in Russian history was much on Karamzin's mind at the beginning of the nineteenth century. His article "Concerning Events and Characters in Russian History Which Can Serve as Subjects of Art" ["O slučaex i xarakterax v russkoj istorii, kotorye mogut byt' predemetom xudožestv"], which appeared shortly before the publication of "Martha," clearly summarizes his intent. Whether it be the Slavs inviting Rurik to rule over them, Svyatoslav refusing to surrender in battle, or Vladimir at the moment of his baptism, Karamzin envisions art as a proper method of commemorating "a monumental era in our [Russian] history," or "a victory which saved the Russian land." [15] In each example he chooses, the subject's straining body and emotions invariably reflect the greater historical event of which he is a part. The idea of uniting art with Russian history did not, of course, originate with Karamzin. Lomonosov had suggested it many years earlier in his "Ideas for Pictorial Scenes From Russian History" ["Idei dlja živopisnyx kartin iz russkoj istorii"] (1764). Karamzin's contribution was to dramatize a sense of the participant's inner psychological state as he experiences a decisive moment in Russia's past. He suggested that the character's inner thoughts and feelings be developed in order to focus attention on the importance of the event itself. [16]

Those principles of joining art to history are embodied in "Martha" as Karamzin, first, defines his characters so that their interest as personae heightens the impact of the national events surrounding Novgorod's resistance and defeat. Second, Karamzin carefully represents those events within their own physical, military, and cultural setting, thereby establishing a sense of the causes and effects associated with the republic's defeat and Martha's death. There is, then, a uniformity of vision here in which characters, together with the rendering of period and locale, are joined to evoke the reader's full appreciation of Russia at a crossroads in its historical development.

There were no viable prose models for the serious historical tale in Russia at the turn of the nineteenth century. The adventure novels of Popov, Chulkov, or Levshin plied the reader with heavy doses of magic and a chain of loosely connected adventures, all overlaid with folk superstition. Their settings, while sometimes Russian in name (Novgorod or Kiev), made no pretense of accuracy in presenting actual historical conditions, issues, or characters. Their appeal was uniformly based on enjoyable fantasy in the manner of Western romances. [17] Karamzin's own "Natalia" points out his earlier idyllic treatment of historical setting and character.

In his attempt to establish a socio-historical basis on which to develop his tale, Karamzin found more help in examining Russian chronicles of the past. [18] To that study he added a serious interest in the *Slovo* as well as a knowledge of the *Byliny* then available to him. [19] Clearly, Karamzin vigorously pursued an acquaintance with authentic Russian sources in setting the stage of Novgorod's destruction. Professor L. V. Krestova in her recent assessment of "Martha" has accumulated a list of names, events and cultural details in the tale which Karamzin mined from such documents. [20] The lengthy debate between Martha and Prince Kholmsky early in the story, for example, develops around an extensive summary of major events in Russia over the preceding seven centuries. But these purely Russian sources are important in the tale in that they lend a rich background which Karamzin manipulates and, at times, alters [21] in order to formulate clearly his vision of the Novgorod question.

To achieve that artistic clarification of history Karamzin composed "Martha" according to a classical heroic or epic design. The opinion of Martha as a character of heroic proportions has often been offered, [22] but usually in a limited sense as a way of referring to her extraordinary zeal or the tale's "lofty" tone and its patriotic message. The heroic elements of the tale are a good deal more important, however, for epic concepts lie at the root of

Karamzin's definition of character, his choice and arrangement of setting and detail, his use of narrative perspectives, and his compositional ordering of the tale.

The "heroic age" of a people violently emerging from energetic disorder into a more stable organization, with its select strong personalities (warrier-heroes), was the domain of epic poetry in the eighteenth century. [23] The central distinction between modern representations of that topic and its ancient models in Homer was the newer emphasis on nationalism rather than personal issues of the heroic definition. The forceful representation of a country's destiny in the making had already been practiced extensively in the West and in Russia. [24] Voltaire's *Henriade* was the archetype in the eighteenth century and Kheraskov's national commemorative, the *Rossijada*, marked the genre's high point in Russia in 1779. Historical tragedies, which shared a number of epic concepts, were equally popular and more abundant (e.g., Marie-Joseph Chénier in France and Ja. B. Knyazhnin in Russia). The heroic vision of national history, epitomized in the epic and tragedy of this period, thrived on the contemporary interest in republican liberty vs. autocratic organization in the West. [25] In her discussion of "Martha" the Soviet critic Ju. F. Florinskaya marshals a good deal of evidence attesting to Karamzin's reliance not only on the historical tragedy but on fine arts (e.g., Létier's "Last Moments of Cato"), and music (e.g., Beethoven's "Ninth Symphony"), all of which share an inspiration from his age's interest in classical models of republicanism. [26] It is in concert with that movement, continues Florinskaya, that Karamzin openly refers to Martha as "the Cato of Novgorod."

The West's (and Russia's) general association of history and art within heroic forms was admirably suited to Karamzin's own intent as enunciated in "Concerning

Events and Characters Which Can Serve as Subjects of Art." As in the epic and historical tragedy, for example, Karamzin's central character in "Martha" is important because of her greater capacity to live and act in accordance with a transcendant obligation. That obligation does not pertain to the epic hero alone (it is shared by his compatriots as well) but its greater concentration in the hero elevates him above his fellows. In Homer, for example, that obligation is one of personal glory; Achilles and his comrades share the urge to gain honor in the exhibition of personal valor during battle. Those desires are simply more concentrated in the central hero. The eighteenth century carried on the same concept of the hero (e.g., Henry IV in the *Henriade* and Ivan III in the *Rossijada)*. What was changed was the criterion of personal glory, its replacement in the eighteenth century being national glory.

Martha and other Novgorodians of noble rank share the same devotion to republican freedom. At times her compatriots approach her dedication to that ideal but it is for Martha to represent the epitome of that characteristic. While less hardy inhabitants of the city vacillate in their zeal to hold out against Moscow's forces, Martha never loses her resolve. Indeed, Karamzin openly equates his heroine with the value of civil freedom in several places. In the see-saw battle with Moscow, she and the war cry of freedom are synonymous ("liberty and Martha designated the same thing in the great city"). For Novgorod, liberty's symbolic destruction is identified with Martha in her death. As she is buried, the freedom bell is removed and Novgorodians "follow it like children following their parents' coffin."

Of course, as epic traditions demanded, Karamzin made a clear distinction in his characters between the select few of noble origin who might aspire to heroic stature and the nameless bulk of the populace, the čern'. Heroes like Ivan III and Prince Kholmsky, or Martha and Miroslav, are individualized as decision makers, unlike their respective armies. The great masses of ordinary characters appear only as groups that react to the events epic heroes create. That distinction is metonymically apparent, for example, in a hero's better and more brilliant armor and apparel.

The heroic manner of presenting characters in a completely extroverted manner is also basic to Karamzin's method. Their inner capacities, motives and goals are unambiguously placed before the reader in the form of objective statement. The secrets or complex inner motives of characters in Karamzin's earlier tales are quite foreign to the heroic design. As its conventions demand, Karamzin draws his characters with crystal clear values and consistent modes of behavior; the epic author clearly and impersonally enunciates each's essential qualities and capacities. [27] What the reader learns about a character from those declarative statements is borne out by his actions, his speech, and finds corroboration in what others say about him in the work.

The epic writer's use of the epithet is a typical device in this respect, for, when associated with the name of a character, it tends to encompass and express economically the whole of his importance in the work. For instance in "Martha" there are:

The terror of Livonia, Georgy the *doughty* [Užas Livonii, Georgij *Smelyj*]

The Conqueror of Vitovta, Vladimir the *illustrious* [Pobeditel' Vitovta, Vladimir *Znamenityj*]

The *fierce* men of Murom, inhabitants of the
dark forests
[*Surovye* muromcy, žiteli temnyx lesov]

Alexander the *illustrious*
[Aleksandr *Znamenityj*]

Mikhail the *brave*
[Mixail *Xrabryj*]

Dmitry the *strong*
[Dmitrij Sil'nyj]

These are secondary characters and, as such, fade in and
out of the narrative, playing minor roles in the events of
the *fabula* and disappearing. They are complete, their
psychological interest for the reader falling symmetrically
within the epithets attached to them. Some characters
tend to have more elaborate epithets. Prince Kholmsky,
for example, is "a man judicious and resolute, the right
hand of Ivan in military undertakings, his eye in affairs of
government, brave in battles, eloquent in counsel."

The central epic hero is traditionally a more complex
character and is the subject of a more thorough definition
than his fellows. The question of fate is particularly strong
in understanding his role in the work and Karamzin makes
extensive use of it in presenting Martha. Omens and predictions, the supernatural heralds of fate, attend these heroes
at important moments in their lives. [28] At her birth,
Martha's cries signal a great military victory over Novgorod's enemies. In the contest between her city and
Moscow, Karamzin draws on the natural world for some
omens (e.g., animals howling in the darkness, flesh-eating
ravens wheeling overhead "as if waiting for a feast soon to

come," and lightning flashing against a dark cloud that covers the sun). But the central omen of doom in "Martha," as in the *Iliad* and most Western heroic poetry, is clearly enunciated in the form of a human voice with a miraculous source. After the bell falls in the city, a voice from the ruins warns 'O Novgorod! Thus will your glory tumble! Thus will your greatness disappear!'". (In Book XIX of the *Iliad*, Achilles's horse Xanthos speaks as a human when he predicts his master's destruction as he returns to battle. In the *Rossijada*, Tsar Ivan III is called upon in a dream to put aside his earlier frivolity and assumed his fated obligation to free Russia from Tatar control.)

Fate is also integral to the larger question of the epic hero as a tragic figure. Here Karamzin's recourse to the Homeric epic (i.e., the *Iliad*) and contemporary historical tragedy is particularly strong (Voltaire's and Kheraskov's *poemas* did not draw their respective heroes as tragic but as successful). The epic hero achieves tragic stature through his conscious choice of acting in a manner destined to destroy him. It is apparent that Achilles is of that category since he decides of his own free will to return to battle after having been warned of the consequences. [29] Martha is drawn in an analogous condition as she, and Novgorod, seek to resist their appointed fate. The hermit Feodosy warns that war will destory the city and Martha knowingly assumes the heroic burden of choosing honor over life when she responds: "The fate of men and nations is the secret of providence, but deeds depend on us alone, and that is enough." As the battle is being fought, Martha again refers to fate: "and let heaven decide our fate!" Even when the war is lost, she acknowledges fate's determination of the matter: "Heaven must decide the life and death of people. Man is free only in his deeds and feelings."

Through his decision, the epic hero becomes associated with a standard which, as he openly acknowledges, transcends his own personality. The archetype for that epic choice in earlier times was personal honor in the eyes of one's fellows. His superior capacity to live, fight, and die in conscious accord with the dictates of glory grant him heroic status. The fact that he consciously chooses such glory over his own life thus makes him tragic. Martha's unyielding sense of obligation to the ideal of Novgorod's freedom is heroic in the same way (in terms of the modern sense of obligation to one's nation). Her conscious act of sacrificing herself and everyone important to her to that cause establishes the same tragic status for her.

Those sections of "Martha" in which the heroine knowingly assumes her obligation are virtually dramatic in formulation and are as easily adaptable to the stage as to prose. Reflecting his age's formal similarities between the epic and historical tragedy, Karamzin has his heroine formalize the ideological position she represents with carefully reasoned arguments. Her speeches are of monolog length and stylistically partake liberally of complex syntax and the oratorical flourishes of clauses built around key repeated words, rhetorical address, personification of abstract concepts, etc.

The opening scenes of the tale are arranged as a dramatized debate between Martha (as the representative of republican autonomy) and Prince Kholmsky (the spokesman for Ivan's vision of civil organization). As in Voltaire's or Kheraskov's *poemas* or Chenier's or Knyazhnin's tragedies, Martha obeys the classical heroic convention of clearly verbalizing her commitment. [30] That commitment in turn leads her to a conflict from which, as discussed above, derives her tragic stature.

Karamzin's psychological portraiture of Martha, with its epic emphasis on issues greater than her own private personality, leaves little room for the intimacies so common in his earlier tales. When personal moments in her or her family's lives do appear they are designed to accentuate her primary obligation. For example, Ksenia and Miroslav marry as a direct result of Martha's plan to consolidate the city's morale prior to the decisive battle with Moscow (his marriage to Martha's daughter legitimizes his leadership of the army). Ksenia grieves for her dead bridegroom after the battle but, following her mother's example, she takes pride in his death as a defender of freedom. Martha is particularly striking in the way she turns personal emotions to the service of her city's cause. On hearing that her own sons are killed in the war with Moscow she responds: "Praise heaven! Fathers and mothers of Novgorod! Now I can comfort you!" She has long since converted her love for her dead husband into the same kind of commitment to protect Novgorodian freedom. As is proper in the epic, the hero has no developed personal biography. Only those facts about his past that pertain to his decisions and actions within the heroic events of the work find their way into his past or present. Details about Martha's private life before the battle for Novgorod are limited to facts that pertain to her resolve to keep her city independent (e.g., her birth with its miracles, or her vow to her husband). The epic hero has few inner motives, but those he does have are unchanging and clearly visible. His personality is fixed as he acts primarily in response to a clear standard (i.e., personal honor or zealous patriotism).

As in both the Homeric epic and historical tragedies, Karamzin builds a serious flaw *(hamartia)* into his heroine which justifies her eventual destruction. That flaw comes from the same source as her tragic greatness. Achilles's wrath leads him to an extreme attitude (i.e., humiliating Agamemnon and his willingness to multilate Hector's body). Consistent with his historical theme, Karamzin, much like Knyazhnin's Vadim in *Vadim Novgorodskij,* transposes Martha's flaw into the charge of "fanaticism" in keeping her city free. She is ready to ruin Novgorod in an attempt to defend it. In each case, the epic hero's greatest asset leads to an excess which causes (or justifies) his downfall. As Northrop Frye points out, the epic hero's "authority, passions, and powers of expression [are] far greater than ours, but what he does is subject to social criticism and to the order of nature." [31]

Karamzin's presentation of Martha, both in her tragic obligation and in her private life, thus exemplifies his theoretical attitude toward historical fiction. She illustrates his intent to "psychologize" characters primarily as they function within an important historical cause which they represent but which also transcends them as private beings. [32]

Like his approach to character, Karamzin's methods of description are firmly rooted in epic conventions. The tale's physical and social context, like its major conflict, emphasizes the heroic potential of a moment in national history. Here Karamzin's interest in developing the compositional potential of neutral omniscient narration coincides with the objectivity and authority long associated with epic narrative conventions. As Erich Auerbach remarks, epic narration aspires "to present phenomena in a fully externalized form, visible and palpable in their parts, and completely fixed in their spatial and temporal relations." [33] That narrative perspective, with its central emphasis on presenting unquestioned facts and fully revealed motives was especially appropriate to Karamzin's task of establishing and clarifying the socio-historical tensions involved in the Novgorod question. Any considerations in description that distract the reader's attention from those issues impede the rapid flow of events that give the epic and Karamzin's historical tale their clarity of composition. [34] For both, the physical context is shaped and described to emphasize the heroic events of the work.

Karamzin's inclusion of large amounts of specific *realia* related to social customs and ranks, religious ceremonies, military information, how important characters' homes are furnished, feasts, funerals, etc., all correspond to epic categories. For example, those details of the city pertaining to political and military aspects of the conflict are much in evidence. The story begins with the ringing of the freedom bell, the calling of the ruling deputies *[posadniki]* together with the military commanders *[tysjačkie]* with their symbolic rods or *žezly*. The elders *[starosty]* (representing each of Novgorod's five sections) all carry their marks of rank (silver pole-axes). When war begins, the guarantees of peace *[kljatvennye gramoty]* are returned to Ivan III. The republic's banner *[xorugv' otečestva]* is brought out on solemn occasions to concentrate the city's attention on their ideal of autonomy. The regions contributing troops to Novgorod's cause are specifically named:

> The inhabitants of the Neva shores, of the great lake Il'men, of Onega, Mologa, Lovat, Shelona, one after the other appeared in the central camp . . .

Further specificity regarding their relationship with the city is supplied by a footnote explaining that these allies come from the five administrative districts of Novgorod:

Vodskaya, Obonezhskaya, Bezhetskaya, Derevskaya, and Shelonskaya.

Military details of trumpets and kettledrums played by "musicians in red silk cloaks" who march at the head of the troops of Novgorod's allies, the ten German city republics, appear in Karamzin's story. They carry presents of gold bars and precious stones on silver trays in symbolic acts of unity and support. Reminiscent of most epics, Karamzin describes armament and preparations for battle, complete with the *topos* of hyperbole amidst a good deal of sensual detail:

> The banners were unfurled, armament thundered
> and shone, the earth groaned with the thudding
> of horses' hooves — and the terrible legions were
> hidden by clouds of dust.

Certain set expressions and comparisons woven into Karamzin's descriptive design freely borrow from those of epic poetry. The Russian is especially inclined to some of Homer's favorite metonymic expressions of violent death on the battlefield which were as popular in eighteenth-century heroic poetry as well (e.g., "his gaze was darkened by a cloud" or "the sword . . . smoked with blood."). One of the most striking conventions of description common to epics, ancient and modern, is the complex or Homeric simile. It is distinctive by its extended vehicle or image, which is rich in verbs and develops into a miniature narration of its own. For example:

> Even as when a goatherd from a place of out-
> look seeth a cloud coming across the deep
> before the blast of the west wind; and to him

> being afar it seemeth ever blacker, even as pitch,
> as it goeth along the deep, and bringeth a great
> whirlwind, and he shuddereth to see it and
> driveth his flock beneath a cave; even in such
> wise moved the serried battalions of young men,
> the fosterlings of Zeus ... (the *Iliad,* Book IV)

Karamzin carefully follows that structure and even the
kind of imagery in a simile devoted to ill-fated Ksenia:

> So does a young innocent shepherd, still illu-
> mined by the sun's rays, look with curiosity at
> the lightning flashing in the distance, not know-
> ing that a terrible cloud on the wings of a storm
> is speeding towards him and will burst upon him
> and strike him down. (Book II)

Within a few paragraphs a second Homeric simile appears,
thereby reinforcing the device's visibility:

> The people accompanied Ksenia, distraught and
> amazed by the sudden change of her fate ... So
> does a young turtle dove, raised under the wing
> of her mother, see her peaceful nest destroyed
> by a storm and in vain would she stand against
> the direction of the gale by the weak efforts of
> her delicate wings. (Book II)

Realia descriptions extend into peaceful cultural
areas as well. As in many epics, there is a description of the
hero's residence. In keeping with the convention, Karamzin concentrates on exactly those characteristics accentuated by the epic author,[35] (i.e., the richness of possessions, as well as their place of origin to emphasize their

uniqueness). Martha's home is "graced with valuable rugs and rich German fabrics; everywhere are lit silver candle-holders." In epic fashion, Martha is described as serving her army an elaborate meal and distributing gifts to the warriors, all of which magnifies her special glory in their eyes. Details of a hero's burial and the description of a graveside oration also appear together with the enumeration of the deceased's glorious deeds in defense of the city *[xartija slavy]*.

The objective enumeration of physical detail and social customs is a feature "Martha" shares with the other late tales ("A Knight" and "The Sensitive and the Cold"). That emphasis on transcribing the specifics of time and place in contemporary or historical Russian society is a consistent feature of Karamzin's experimentation with the more extensive use of third person (neutral omniscient) narration. His growing interest in national history, which is soon to engross him in his *History of the Russian State [Istorija gosudarstva rossijskago]*, in part also reflects that same bent toward accumulating and arranging a wide spectrum of cultural data to capture the essence of the time described.

Karamzin's adaptation of heroic conventions to make vivid formative events in his nation's past extends to his use of the intruding author device as well as to those elements of "Martha" discussed above. He turns the device's traditional potential for both clarifying abstract ideas and imposing opinions on the reader to the tasks he sets for himself in writing historical fiction (i.e., the isolation of important events in national history and their presentation as exciting in terms of the participants' experiences).

In his preface to the tale Karamzin assumes a judgmental posture, superior to the work's actual events, from which he clarifies the contest between Novgorod and Moscow. He leaves no room for contradiction in his justification of Moscow's legitimacy as conqueror: "Wise Ivan had to join Novgorod's territory to his control for the glory and strength of the homeland: glory to him!" He is editorially eager to honor the Novgorodians for their courage in maintaining their ideal of autonomy. ("The Novgorodians' resistance was not the rebellion of some Jacobins. . ."), but he passes sentence on their cause, given Russia's historical need to consolidate its regions under a single ruler.

Within the text of the tale proper Karamzin interjects another kind of authorial remark disguised as the voice of the ancient author of the manuscript (the equivalent of the epic bard). In this form, editorial comment is more commemorative than explanatory. Like the traditional bard who at times appears *in propria persona* within his own production, Karamzin "sings" a hymn of praise to the contest's solemn grandeur and to the larger issue of national greatness. In this respect, Karamzin's authorial interruptions approach that kind of historical celebration characteristic of the *Henriade* or the *Rossijada*. There is, for example, an apostrophe to Russian valor in battle:

> Deeds glorious and grand! Only Russians, on both sides, could thus wage battle, could thus conquer and be conquered.

To emphasize the magnanimity of the Russian character (Ivan has pardoned the Novgorodian insurgents except for Martha) Karamzin, in the voice of the fictional chronicler of the event, renders the following encomium to his nation:

Clemency! Clemency! joyfully repeated the
Muscovy troops: it seemed that clemency had
been given *them,* so noble are Russians!

The heroic narrative foci of describing things and
people in an extroverted manner, and the heroic author's
remarks *in propria persona* fitted Karamzin's avowed
emphases in the historical tale nicely. The first provided a
model for the objective presentation of actual cultural and
political facts which the Russian wished to incorporate
into his tale. The model of an epic author commenting on
certain aspects of his work was also admirably suited to
Karamzin's attempt both to clarify the historical perspective of Novgorod's resistance to Ivan III, and to lend his
tale the solemnity of tone that that momentous conflict
implied in Russia's national growth.

Finally, "Martha" owes much to heroic conventions
in its general compositional format. Karamzin divides his
tale into books, each of which is in turn composed of
distinct scenic episodes. Each episode is based on a running
alternation between impersonal description (neutral
omniscient narration) and highly structured monologs
delivered by the characters, and punctuated periodically
by the effusive exclamations of the zealous "bard" or
chronicler. Battle episodes and views of armed camps
alternate with domestic scenes and the formal monologs of
debate or heated negotiations among allies. The epic's
composition, so usable for presenting a historical crisis in
its military, political, social and personal facets, was admirably suited to Karamzin's purpose.

By his adaptation of earlier literary forms Karamzin
succeeded in creating an engaging representation of Novgorodian life and values typical of the fifteenth century.

Equally important, he succeeded in producing a rounded assessment of an important moment in his country's formation, complete with its causes and effects. As a result, he was the first Russian to render the "body and pressure" of an age in his national past against a believable cultural background. Karamzin's heroine, while attractive for her personal qualities, takes on greatest meaning as she relates to a larger issue (political and military) of her time. A solid basis of social causation molds her actions and determines her heroic stature in the work. Reliance on the epic compositional structure with its episodic divisions and varied scenes of war and peace, helped him to place his heroic characters in their physical and cultural ethos. By mastering and coordinating the diverse elements of epic poetry, as well as their reflection in historical drama, Karamzin succeeded in creating the first Russian modern historical fiction worthy of the name.

Conclusion

To trace the development of Karamzin's narrative prose is to follow a significant stage of Russia's emergence into its literary independence. Bridging the eighteenth and nineteenth centuries, Karamzin was most adept at crystallizing the West's mature esthetic accomplishments in his own clear and striking images. Histories of Russian literature rarely neglect to point out his debt to Richardson, Sterne, Thomson, Macpherson, Rousseau, Marmontel, Gessner, etc. In large part Karamzin's vision of what is important in man, what is beautiful in his world, and what pursuits are worthy of his commitment, was inspired directly by those foreign predecessors. Moreover, the vigorous growth and change of his own world view led him to resort to different foreign masters at each stage of his own maturing talent. There is adequate contemporary discussion of Karamzin's literary evolution to counter the more traditional view that his literary niche is limited to that of a "sweet" sentimentalist, a spinner of passive and melancholy moods.

Karamzin remained convinced of Russia's need to merge its own literary fortunes with those of Europe — his own version of "cosmopolitanism." His concept of that mixture consistently reflects two goals. One is his desire to accelerate Russia's movement toward full inclusion within the pale of Western European ideas and esthetics. The second reveals his diligent attempt to stimulate a sense of national identity among Russian writers which would enrich that European community through Russia's presence. Karamzin well understood that his country had a great deal of catching up to do with the West. For awhile, Russia would have to receive more advantages of foreign literary achievements than it could offer in return by way of its own accomplishments. But Karamzin was convinced that his country's *literati* would emerge eventually with an original contribution to the greater Western community.

His speech before the Imperial Russian Academy in 1818 speaks directly to the needs he himself experienced as an author. He said, first:

> Unique beauty, which constitutes the character of national literature, yields to general beauty; the first is subject to change, the second is eternal. It is good to write for Russians but it is still better to write for all people. If it is demeaning for us to walk behind others, then we can walk along side them toward the universal goal of mankind. . .

Then, with the next breath, he affirmed:

> Resembling Europeans in many ways we yet differ from them in certain talents, customs and

skills, . . . We can relate this truth to literature as well. Being the mirror of the national mind and heart, it also must have in it something special which is unnoticed in a single author, but which is obvious in them [national authors] as a whole. Having the taste of the French, we have our own special taste as well.

More than any of his contemporaries Karamzin provided a variety of excellent examples for that proposed literary interaction with the West. "Poor Liza" affirms the Rousseauian concept of emotional and spiritual sensitivity in simple people of a low social class. In its rhythmical syntax and its evocative euphonic patterns, it emphasizes the imagination of the story-teller's own warm personality and thereby fits the growing Western interest in the intimate narrator. "Julia" relies on Marmontel's earlier exploration of the society tale with its emphasis on inner psychological conflicts played out against a recognizable social backdrop. "Bornholm Island" develops around a core of Ossianic situations, character types and description methods. "My Confession" articulates on an openly acknowledged debt to Rousseau's own *Confessions.* "Martha the Mayoress" owes its basic compositional form and its definition of characters to the heroic tradition of the age. Often adapting his borrowings to the Russian scene, Karamzin was the first of his countrymen to transplant Western themes, characters and locales to believably Russian soil. As Veselovsky and Simmons point out, Russian readers in the early nineteenth century justifiably revered Karamzin as the most talented adapter of foreign literature to his own national scene.

In another and equally valid sense, however, Karamzin represents the beginning of an independent growth in

Russian prose which was to follow him and be inspired by him. The popularity he received for his evocation of tears over "poor Liza's fate," or his painting of Russia's heroic national past in "Martha," continued unabated for more than a generation after their first appearance. Even the parodies visited upon Karamzin's Lizas and Natalias, an inevitable result of all the lesser Russian talents who imitated him, speak eloquently of the earlier impact and influence exercised by those characters. Critics can justifiably approach Karamzin's prose as a self-sustaining body of ideas and their formal implementation. His work represents a crucial moment of transition for Russian prose in which foreign influences were transformed into a viable body of national literature. Admittedly, Karamzin wrote in response to established values and forms of the West. To a significant extent, however, successive generations of Russia's writers were to compose in response to the values and forms of Karamzin.

It has been the purpose of this study to discuss Karamzin's narrative art primarily in terms of itself, as a corpus of work worthy of analysis in its own right. The questions it has sought to raise are twofold: first, what intrinsic coherence is there between ideational and formal qualities in each work considered; second, what patterns of evolution mark those qualities in his prose over the twelve-year period discussed here. Central to this inquiry has been the criterion of narrative point of view. Karamzin's choice of narrative perspective not only organizes the text structure of a given work, it is a sensitive index to his pronounced evolution in subject matter and in general formal technique. The chronological study of his altered narrative vision clarifies greatly the Russian's maturation as thinker and artist.

Karamzin's early prose — the *Letters* and his first

tales — are cohesive in their representation of sentimental principles. The prominence of the intruding author is an explanatory presence in those works; it constantly serves the didactic task of recommending those principles to the reader. When Karamzin assumes the personalized stance of a narrator, he consistently reinforces those same principles on an emotional, experiential basis. The rhetorical potential of arguing for a system of values on the general level while bringing those same values to life as particularized examples characterized much of the West's prose of the eighteenth century from moral tracts to sermons to novels. That rhetorical tradition found a talented reformulation in Russia via Karamzin's early prose.

The *Letters* and the early tales maintain Karamzin's sturdy faith in a sentimental system of moral and esthetic ideals. They stress positive alternatives to vulgar everyday life or they promise a better life to come, all of which is well served by the admonishing presence of the intruding author. In Karamzin's middle prose tales there simultaneously appear more pessimistic themes and a new concentration on a character-narrator. His emotional involvement with plot events and his limited cognition of what those events mean coincide with each piece's thematic emphasis on destroyed personal hope. The result is a growing sense of moral instability which argues with the optimism of the early works. Passive sorrow, the characteristic mood of the narrator in "Bornholm Island," yields to active revolt against life in the narrator of "Sierra Morena." That qualitative change from quiet disillusionment to overt despair in theme parallels the status of the narrator as one increasingly involved in the events he describes. The second cycle ends with "My Confession" which carries the vision of moral instability to its extreme. Through numerous examples, the hero-narrator reveals his total alienation from all moral values (many of which had figured earlier in Karamzin's prose). He is quite comfortable in a relativist existence where his own personal caprice is the only goal worth pursuing. Symptomatically, his narrative perspective is more involuted than those of the preceding narrator-characters.

In his last works Karamzin again attempts to construct an artistic sense of coherent stability in man's life which bespeaks a renaissance of his optimism as a writer. It is a changed and more practical sort of stability, however. His characters do not relate primarily to any elusive set of sentimental or moral abstractions, but to the objective facts and mores of their own psyches and their own society. In his last tales Karamzin poses the central question of how an individual grows emotionally and intellectually in a given social environment. At first he experiments with the contemporary Russian milieu as a means of investigating that relationship. Both "A Knight of Our Time" and "The Sensitive and the Cold" dwell on the question of how modern man matures, how he accommodates the values which typify his social ambiance. Whether it be Locke's theory of developmental psychology (in "A Knight") or its opposite (the concept of unalterable inborn potential in "The Sensitive and the Cold"), Karamzin keeps his attention trained on the basic premise that the psychic mass of an individual necessarily assumes distinct form in accordance with the limits his society poses for him. In "Martha," Karamzin varies his search for links of influence by resorting to the perspective of Russian history. He draws his major characters as personally defined by the opposed social philosophies of their time. As those causes come into conflict and find a resolution, his characters (Martha most of all) grow as personalities. Martha's complexity as a person, her strengths as well as her weaknesses, reveal a great deal about the social cause she supports.

Karamzin's primary interest in his last tales is neither didactic (unlike the first cycle of tales) nor does it seek to evoke isolated, intensely emotional states of mind (as in the second cycle). He seeks rather to describe the myriad subtle means by which the values and manners of a society relate to the personalities of its constituent members. As a result, third person narration (neutral omniscience) is employed to a degree not visible in his earlier tales. The mode's capacity to enumerate unargued facts and detail admirably fits his central task of description. To clarify the metonymic texture of his late prose ("A Knight" and "The Sensitive and the Cold") he periodically employs the more traditional intruding author to consolidate the mass of single facts about his characters which appears in neutral omniscience. In "Martha," Karamzin relies on traditional heroic methods of narrative technique to assess his historical characters as well as to arrange the cultural, military and political detail associated with Novgorod's republican position. That same heroic tradition also answered Karamzin's intention of rendering editorial opinion about the meaning of both characters and historical context within the evolution of his nation.

Karamzin occupies a prominent place in any discussion of Russia's development of a modern national literature. More than any other Russian prose author of his time, he adapted Western ideas and esthetics perceptively and subtly to meet the growing sophistication of his country's reading public. As apparent as that adaptation, when it is sought, is his considerable talent as an independent thinker and artist. The progress of his growth, along with his eclectic use of Western literary traditions, is clearly visible in the formal structure of his prose works. In particular, his evolving choice of narrative point of view graphically reveals the dynamics of his artistic development.

Notes

Notes to Introduction

[1] For example, see D. D. Blagoj, "Puškin i russkaja literatura XVIII v.," *Puškin, rodonačal'nik novoj russkoj literatury* (Ak. Nauk, 1941), pp. 152-155 for a brief description of Karamzin's influence on Pushkin.

[2] See J. G. Garrard, "Karamzin in Recent Soviet Criticism: A Review," *Slavic and East European Journal,* V. XI, No. 4 (1967), pp. 464-472 for a contemporary discussion of critical attention to Karamzin.

[3] See Henry M. Nebel, *N. M. Karamzin: A Russian Sentimentalist* (Mouton and Co., 1967) and Anthony G. Cross,

N. M. Karamzin: A Study of His Literary Career (1783-1802) (Southern Illinois, 1971).

[4]See Lionel Trilling, "Manners, Morals, and the Novel," *Approaches to the Novel,* ed. Robert Scholes (San Francisco, 1961), p. 232.

[5]See Wayne C. Booth, *The Rhetoric of Fiction* (University of Chicago Press, 1961), chap. I.

[6]Lubomír Doležel, "The Typology of the Narrator: Point of View in Fiction," *To Honor Roman Jakobson,* 3 vols. (Mouton, 1967), I, p. 544.

[7]See Norman Friedman, "Point of View in Fiction: The Development of a Critical Concept," *Approaches to the Novel,* (1961), pp. 113-142.

[8]See I. Z. Sherwood, "The Novelists as Commentators," *The Age of Johnson: Essays Presented to C. B. Tinker* (Yale University Press, 1949), pp. 116-117.

[9]*Ibid.,* p. 113.

[10]*Ibid.,* p. 119.

[11]Friedman, p. 130.

[12]See Bertil Romberg, *Studies in the Technique of the First Person Novel* (Stockholm, 1962), p. 94.

[13]See Robie Macauley and George Lanning, *Technique in Fiction* (new York, 1964), p. 109.

Notes to Chapter One

[1]The publication of the *Letters* was a rather involved affair. The first half (up to the author's arrival in Paris) was published between 1791-1792 in Karamzin's own *Moscow Journal*. The rest appeared irregularly in later editions of his travel notes. It was only in 1801 that the complete text of the *Letters* was published. A. G. Cross, in his excellent book *N. M. Karamzin: A Study of His Literary Career (1783-1803)*, pages 66-68, provides an informative synopsis of the work's publication and Karamzin's problems with the repressive censorship policies of Paul's reign in the 1790s. His explanation that the *Letters* was essentially completed by 1794 helps explain the work's sense of compositional unity, despite its protracted printing dates.

[2]S. I. Porfir'ev, in his *Istorija russkoj slovesnosti*, č. II, otdel 3 (Kazan, 1891), p. 35, emphasizes Karamzin's pioneering role in opening the Russian mind to the development of modern Western thought and customs when he says: "Through his letters from abroad Karamzin was the first to introduce reliable information about European civilization into our literature."

[3]See T. Roboli, "Literatura 'putešestvij'," *Russkaja proza*, eds. B. Éjxenbaum i Ju. Tynjanov (Mouton, 1963), p. 57 for a short list of travel notes by later Russian writers inspired by Karamzin's *Letters*.

[4]See Karamzin's article "Čto nužno avtoru," *N. M. Karamzin — izbrannye sočinenija* 2 VV., (Moscow, 1964), II, 120-122 concerning his demands for the writer's personal purity as a prerequisite for the writing task.

[5]For a summary of the philosophical and esthetic principles that characterized Western sentimentalism see W. J. Bate, *From Classic to Romantic: Premises of Taste in Eighteenth-Century England* (Harvard University Press, 1946), chaps. IV-VI and H. G. Schenk, *The Mind of the European Romantics* (New York, 1968), chaps. I-II.

[6]See I. Z. Serman, "Zaroždenie romana v russkoj literature XVIII veka," *Istorija russkogo romana,* I (Ak. Nauk, 1962), p. 50.

[7]Some examples are F. A. Émin's *Pis'ma Ernesta i Doravry [Letters of Ernest and Doravra]* (1766), or P. Ju. L'vov's *Rossijskaja Pamela [A Russian Pamela]* (1789).

[8]See V. V. Sipovskij, *Očerki iz russkogo romana,* I, č. 2 [XVIII vek](St. Petersburg, 1910), p. 426.

[9]For example V. V. Vinogradov, in his *Ocerki po istorii russkogo literaturnogo jazyka* (Leiden, 1950), pp. 152-157, discusses the common practice among Russian writers in the eighteenth century of relying heavily on barbarisms, calques and literal translations from foreign languages to convey concepts and feelings for which no Russian equivalents existed.

[10]See V. V. Sipovskij, *N. M. Karamzin, avtor "Pisem russkogo putešestvennika"* (St. Petersburg, 1899), p. 375.

[11]Mikhail Pogodin, in his *N. M. Karamzin,* č. I (Moscow, 1866), like most nineteenth-century critics, took Karamzin's image of spontaneous correspondent in the *Letters* all too seriously (e.g., see pages 95, 106, 142 and

165). Sipovsky, on page 157 of his *Karamzin, avtor. . .* , is careful to point out that the *Letters* was not merely the sum total of Karamzin's letters to his friends the Pleshcheevs. He takes the position that the travel notes form a tightly organized whole, less the spontaneous "mirror of Karamzin's soul" as Pogodin assets (page 165), than a serious literary project which he subjected to four editions and over two thousand textual alterations.

[12]L. N. Timofeev is typical of the many Soviet scholars who persist in schematically juxtaposing Karamzin's psychological, "introverted" narrator and Radishchev's "realistic" narrator who avoids psychological self-analysis in favor of describing actual social conditions. See L. N. Timofeev, "Realism v russkoj literature XVIII veka," *Problemy realizma v russkoj literature,* ed. N. K. Gudzij (Ak. Nauk, 1940), p. 65. See V. V. Vinogradov, *Problema avtorstva i teorija stilej* (Moscow, 1961), pp. 232-238 for a rejoinder to this entrenched tendency to polarize Karamzin's and Radishchev's works.

[13]See N. S. Tixonravov, *Sočinenija,* 3 vols. (Moscow, 1898), III, č. I, p. 311. Sipovsky, in his *Karamzin, avtor. . .* , p. 238, cites a case in which Karamzin's description of a waterfall on the Rhine is actually a close translation of another description by the eighteenth-century British traveler, Moore.

[14]*N. M. Karamzin — izbrannye sočinenija,* 2 vols. (Moscow, 1964), I, 131. All references to the text of the text of the *Letters* are from this edition and will appear in text with appropriate pagination.

[15]See V. V. Vinogradov's discussion of the second

person singular pronoun in *Russkij jazyk* (Moscow, 1948), p. 456.

[16]See Meyer H. Abrams, *The Mirror and the Lamp* (New York, 1953), p. 238.

[17]See D. D. Blagoj, *Istorija russkoj literatury XVIII veka* (Moscow, 1951), p. 513.

[18]See E. G. Kovalevskaja, "Inojazyčnaja leksika v proizvedenijax N. M. Karamzina," *Materialy i issledovanija po leksike russkogo jazyka,* I (Ak. Nauk, 1949), p. 8.

[19]See T. A. Ivanova, "Upotreblenie pričastij v rannix proizvedenijax N. M. Karamzina," *Materialy i issledovanija po leksike russkogo jazyka XVIII veka* (Ak. Nauk, 1965), p. 250.

[20]See E. Stanevič, *Rassuždenie o russkom jazyke,* č. II, (Moscow, 1809), p. 75.

[21]See V. V. Vinogradov, *Očerki po istorii russkogo literaturnogo jazyka,* pp. 168-169.

[22] Dmitrij Čiževskij, in his *On Romanticism in Slavic Literatures* (Mouton, 1957), p. 15, dwells on this description of a waterfall to emphasize how unemotional Karamzin and other eighteenth-century Russian writers could be. Čiževskij then juxtaposes that treatment to a later, romantic presentation of a waterfall (by Boratynsky) to make the difference more obvious.

[23]The rational, Western neo-classical approach to

nature is comprehensively treated by Wimsatt and Brooks in their *Literary Criticism: A Short History* (New York, 1965), chap. 13, and by Bate in his *From Classic to Romantic,* chaps. I-III. Čiževskij provides a helpful synopsis of how Russian literature of the eighteenth century adopted a similarly detached view of nature in his *Outline of Comparative Slavic Literature — Survey of Slavic Civilization,* I (Boston, 1952).

[24]Speaking about the history of the device, in his *Poetic Diction,* Quayle traces it back to Horace, saying that it survived to play an important role in British eighteenth-century poetry. Cicely Davies treats the question at length as a feature of general Western esthetics in his article "Ut Pictura Poesis," *The Modern Language Review,* XXX (1935), pp. 159-169.

[25]N. M. Karamzin, "Otčego v Rossii malo avtorskix talantov," *N. M. Karamzin — izbrannye sočinenij,* (1964), II:184.

[26]*Ibid.,* 187.

[27]"Reč' proiznesennaja na toržestvennom sobranii imperatorskoj rossijskoj akademii," *N. M. Karamzin — izbrannye sočinenij* (1964), II:238.

[28]*Ibid.,* 239. As Karamzin optimistically assesses Russia's future literary talent: "A kto rožden s izbytkom vnutrennix sil, tot i nyne, načav podražaniem, svojstvennym junoj slabosti, budet nakonec *sam soboju* — ostavit' putevoditelej, i svobodnyj dux ego, kak orel derznovennyj, uedinenno vosparit v gornix prostranstvax" ["And who-

ever is born with a surplus of inner strength will, after
having begun with emulation which is appropriate for the
young in his weakness, at last *by himself,* will leave his
guides behind. His free spirit, like a daring eagle, will wheel
alone in the airy spaces of the mountains"]. Given Karamzin's cherished hope of teaching Russian writers how to
follow Western models it is not surprising that his special
talent as a writer lay in his ability to emulate its writers by
using their sentimental themes and literary techniques.
A. N. Veselovsky, in his *Žukovskij, poezija čuvstva; ser-*
dečnago voobraženija (St. Petersburg, 1904) (especially on
page 42) emphasizes his talented and imaginative adher-
ence to hallowed sentimental principles, congratulating
him on being immensely more qualified in that task than
the majority of Russian authors who followed him. E. J.
Simmons, in his *English Literature and Culture in Russia*
(Harvard University Press, 1935) (especially pages
161-203) is typical of the many commentators, including
Veselovsky, who have traced major themes in the *Letters*
back to the best-known figures of eighteenth-century Western literature. Sipovsky makes the point that, although
many of the names and themes of sentimentalism were
sporadically found in Russia before Karamzin, the latter
had the effect of greatly clarifying those influences and
fanning the spark of sensibility into full flame. See
Sipovsky, *Karamzin, avtor . . .,* pages 453, 456, 550. N. D.
Kochetkova, in her "Idejno-literaturnye pozicii masonov
80-90-x godov XVIII v. i N. M. Karamzin," *XVIII vek,*
sbornik 6 (Moscow-Leningrad, 1964), pages 197-223, has
demonstrated Karamzin's reliance on many established
sentimental ideals common to the Masonic movement in
Moscow of the late eighteenth century (e.g., spiritual
equality among the classes, the value of friendship, faith in
an after life, etc.).

²⁹See T. Roboli, "Literatura 'putešestvij'," *Russkaja proza*, p. 50.

³⁰See Pogodin's discussion of the Journal's composition on pages 170-171 of his *N. M. Karamzin*, č. I.

Notes to Chapter Two

¹ See D. D. Blagoj, *Istorija russkoj literatury v trex tomax*, I, pp. 632-633.

² See Pogodin, *N. M. Karamzin*, č. I, p. 205.

³ See Sipovsky, *Očerki...*, I, č. 2, pp. 410-421 for his resumé of various critical articles in Russia that indicate domestic familiarity with the West's preoccupation with love involving social obstacles.

⁴ See Pogodin, *N. M. Karamzin*, č. I, p. 203.

⁵ All references to "Poor Liza" are from *N. M. Karamzin — izbrannye sočinenija* (1964), I.

⁶ See B. Éjxenbaum, "Karamzin," *Skvoz' literaturu* (Leningrad, 1921), pp. 47-48.

⁷ L. I. Kulakov, on page 151 of his "Éstetičeskie vzgljady N. M. Karamzina," *Russkaja literatura XVIII veka — époxa klassicizma*, points out that the very musicality of Karamzin's syntax carried the author's aspiration to present directly man's illusive spirit, beyond the isolated semantic meaning of each word.

[8] See G. A. Gukovskij, *Russkaja literatura XVIII veka* (Moscow, 1939), p. 507; and K. Skipina, "O čuvstvitel' noj povesti," *Russkaja proza,* esp. pp. 18-28, for a more detailed discussion of Karamzin's euphonic effects in his prose.

[9] V. D. Levin, on page 199 of his *Kratkij očerk istorii russkogo literaturnogo jazyka* (Moscow, 1958), takes Karamzin to task for the euphonic elegance of his sentence structure, faulting it on its distance from the conversational style of contemporary Russian speech.

[10] See E. N. Kuprejanova, "Russkij roman pervoj četverti XIX veka. Ot sentimental'noj povesti k romanu," *Istorija russkogo romana,* I, p. 71 for a brief discussion of the interrelation between character psychology and moral lessons as practiced in Russian fiction of the eighteenth century. The definitive work on Russian novels of this period is still Sipovsky's *Očerki . . . .*

[11] See Sipovskij, *Očerki . . . ,* I, č. 2, p. 410.

[12] See Ju. D. Levin, "Anglijskaja prosvetitel'skaja žurnalistika v russkoj literature XVIII veka," *Époxa prosveščenija,* ed. M. P. Alekseev (Ak. Nauk, 1967), pp. 3-80, esp. p. 79.

[13] All references to "Natalia" come from *N. M. Karamzin — izbrannye sočinenija* (1964), I.

[14] See W. C. Booth, "The Self-Conscious Narrator in Comic Fiction Before *Tristram Shandy,*" *PMLA,* LXVII (March, 1952), pp. 165, 170.

15 See Henri Fluchére, *Lawrence Sterne: From Tristram to Yorick* (London-New York, 1965), p. 41.

16 W. C. Booth, *The Rhetoric of Fiction*, p. 177.

17 A. A. Mendilow, on page 75 of his *Time and the Novel* (New York, 1965), records Lamb's caustic remarks concerning the manipulative design beneath Sterne's comic digressions:

> An intelligent reader finds a sort of insult in being told, I will teach you how to think upon this subject. This fault ... is a ten-thousandth worse degree to be found in Sterne and many, many modern poets, who continually put a sign-post up to show you where you are to feel. They set out with the assumption their readers to be stupid.

18 John Traugott, *Tristram Shandy's World* (Berkeley, 1954), p. 71.

19 As V. I. Maslov explains on page 355 of his "Interes k Sternu v russkoj literature konca XVIII i načala XIX vv," *Istorika-literaturnyj sbornik, posvjaščennyj V. I. Sreznevskomu* (Leningrad, 1924), Sterne aroused more interest in Russia of the late eighteenth century as a moral philosopher than as a practicing novelist.

20 Fluchére, p. 92.

21 See A. I. Efimov, "Fraziologičeskij sostav povesti Karamzina 'Natal 'ja bojarskaja doč' '," *Materialy i issledo-*

vanija po istorii russkogo literaturnogo jazyka, I (Ak. Nauk, 1949), pp. 83-92. P. N. Polevoj, on page 455 of his *Istorija Russkoj literatury* (St. Petersburg, 1872), speaks with admiration of Karamzin's graceful blending of recognizable Russian phrases with Western "poetic" expressions.

[22] Karamzin's long-term attempt to draw Russian culture into the mainstream of European thought and esthetics is also a consideration in his synthesis of Russian and Western phraseology. By placing uniquely Russian items in close syntactic proximity to standard Western phrases he helped legitimize the former for literary Russian.

[23] All references to "The Beautiful Princess" are from *Sočinenija Karamzina,* 3 vols (St. Petersburg, 1848), II.

[24] See Ju. M. Sokolov, *Russkij fol 'klor* (Moscow, 1938), p. 295.

[25] See Sipovskij, *Očerki* . . . , I, č. 2, pp. 8-22 for a brief outline of the Western knightly romance and its appearance in Russia during the eighteenth century.

[26] See Sipovskij, *Očerki* . . . , I, č. 2, pp. 375-410 for his discussion of how several elements of the romance novel of adventure were altered to meet the new emphases of sentimentalism.

[27] All references to "Julia" are from *Sočinenija Karamzina* (1848).

[28] See Nebel, pp 141-144.

[29] On page 410 of his *Očerki* . . . , I, č. 2, Sipovsky states the nature of that "new moralism" as follows:

> It was expressed in the forceful demand that moral admonitions be hidden. Avoiding too open a didacticism, the reader was to be given the opportunity of receiving firm directives covertly, in the actions [of the characters].

[30] See D. S. Mirsky, *A History of Russian Literature* (New York, 1949), p. 60.

Notes to Chapter Three

[1] See Mixail Pogodin's *N. M. Karamzin po ego sočinenijam, pis'mam i otzyvam sovremennikov*, c.I (Moscow, 1866) pp. 210-265.

[2] See G. Makogonenko, *N. M. Karamzin — izbrannye socinenija*, 2 VV, I, pp. 33-36.

[3] All references to "Bornholm Island" are taken from *N. M. Karamzin — izbrannye sočinenija* (1964), I.

[4] See Earl Kroeber, *Romantic Narrative Art* (University of Wisconsin Press, 1960), p. 188.

[5] See Kroeber, page 77, for a discussion of the

allegorical value of the journey motif and its popularity within romanticism generally.

[6]All references to "Sierra Morena" are taken from *N. M. Karamzin — izbrannye sočinenija* (1964), I.

[7]In her study of "Sierra Morena" the Soviet critic L. V. Krestova points out Karamzin's extensive use of Western models for the general fabula of this tale including M. G. Lewis' *Ambrosio or the Monk* (1795) together with Burger's *Lenore* and Schiller's *Der Geisterseher*. See L. V. Krestova, "Povest' N. M. Karamzina 'Sierra-Morena'," *Rol' i značenie literatury XVIII veka v istorii russkoj kul'tury*, pp. 261-266, esp. p. 262.

[8]All references to "My Confession" come from *N. M. Karamzin — izbrannye sočinenija* (1964), I.

[9]Cross makes the remark on page 129 of his *N. M. Karamzin . . .*, that the Count " . . . is a satire of fashionable gentry education with its abuse of opportunities."

[10]See F. Z. Kanunova's article "Évoljucija sentimentalizma Karamzina ('Moja ispoved' ')," *Rol' i značenie literatury XVIII veka v istorii russkoj kul'tury*, pages 286-290, esp. pp. 287-288, for the most recent Soviet contention of Karamzin's moral intent behind his portrait of Count N. N.

[11]The fact that Stavrogin bites the governor's ear recalls the Count's similar action in biting the Pope's foot and suggests the possibility that Dostoevsky used Karamzin's hero in part as a model for his own character.

^{12}As Krestova points out on page 261 of her article "Povest' N. M. Karamzina 'Sierra-Morena'," "Sierra Morena" originally carried the subtitle "An Elegiac fragment from the Papers of N." *[Elegičeskij otryvok iz bumag N.].*

Notes to Chapter Four

^{1}Timofeev, *Problemy realizma v russkoj literature XVIII veka,* pp. 65-66.

^{2}*Ibid.,* p. 66

^{3}See Pogodin, *N. M. Karamzin,* č. I, pp. 278, 282, 284-285.

^{4}*Ibid.,* p. 328.

^{5}"Reč', proiznesennaja na toržestvennom sobranii imperatorskoj Rossijskoj akademii," *N. M. Karamzin — izbrannye sočinenija* (1964), II, p. 287.

^{6}*Ibid.,* p. 283.

^{7}All references to "A Knight of Our Time" come from *N. M. Karamzin — izbrannye sočinenija* (1964), I.

^{8}Tuveson, pp. 259-260.

^{9}Dmitrij Čiževskij, *Comparative Outline of Slavic*

Literatures, tr. R. N. Porter and M. P. Rice (Vanderbilt University Press, 1971), p. 153.

[10]The question strikes close to Karamzin's own opinions on the value to be derived from reading fiction. See his article "O knižnoj torgovle i ljubvi ko čteniju v Rossii," *N. M. Karamzin – izbrannye sočinenija* (1964), II, pp. 176-180.

[11]All references to "The Sensitive and the Cold" come from *N. M. Karamzin – izbrannye sočinenija*(1964), I.

[12]As Cross points out on page 127 of his *N. M. Karamzin: ...,* this sort of juxtaposition of character types had been made popular earlier in the West by Rousseau in his creation of Saint Preux (the sensitive) and Wolmar (the cold) in *La Nouvelle Héloïse.*

[13]Makogonenko, *N. M. Karamzin – izbrannye sočinenija* (1964), I, p. 48.

[14]All references to "Martha the Mayoress" come from *N. M. Karamzin – izbrannye sočinenija* (1964), I.

[15]*N. M. Karamzin – izbrannye sočinenija,* II (1964), p. 193.

[16]*Ibid.,* p. 194. See also T. S. Karlova's discussion of Karamzin's more serious attitude toward history on page 287 of her article, "Éstetičeskij smysl istorii v tvorčeskom vosprijatii Karamzina," *XVIII vek,* VIII (Ak. Nauk, 1969).

[17]See I. Z. Serman, "Zaroždenie romana v russkoj

literature XVIII veka," *Istorija russkogo romana,* I, pp. 52-59 for a general discussion of the Russian historical novel in the eighteenth century.

[18]As Karamzin wrote to his friend I. I. Dmitriev (May, 1800), "When I sleep I see Nikon with Nestor."

[19]As early as 1794 Karamzin had written a narrative poem ("Ilja Muromec") in imitation of the *Byliny,* with a *bogatyr'* hero and his own version of folk meter. In 1802 he had read and encouraged the publication of A. F. Yakubovich's manuscript of Kirsha Danilov's *Byliny.* For a discussion of Karamzin's contact with Yakubovich's manuscript, see *Drevnie rossijskie stixotvorenija sobrannye Kirseju Danilovym,* ed. D. S. Lixačev (Ak. Nauk, 1958), pp. 513-514.

[20]See L. V. Krestova, "Drevnerusskaja povest' kak odin iz istočnikov povestej .M. Karamzina 'Rajskaja ptička,' 'Ostrov Borngol'm,' 'Marfa posadnica' (iz istorii rannego russkogo romantizma)," *Issledovanija i materialy po drevnerusskoj literature* (Ak. Nauk, 1961), pp. 215-216, 222-224 for specific chronicle and old Russian literary sources in "Martha."

[21]As Professor Krestova points out on pages 217 and 225 of her article "Drevnerusskaja povest'...," Karamzin made substantive changes in Martha's character from accounts appearing in actual chronicles. Instead of their representation of her as a self-serving, personally ambitious woman, Karamzin makes her a "flaming patroit," selfless and honorable in defending the "abstract republicanism" of her city. A direct alteration of historical fact is present in Karamzin's having Martha executed in the

tale rather than her actual fate of being taken alive to Moscow at the close of the war.

[22]See D. D. Blagoj, *Istorija russkoj literatury XVIII veka*, pp. 541-542.

[23]For a fuller discussion of what historical conditions lend themselves to epic representation see L. Abercrombie, *The Epic: An Essay* (London, 1922), pp. 7-13.

[24]As C. Gayley and B. Kurtz say on page 427 of their book *Methods and Materials of Literary Criticism* (Boston, 1920), "From Hegel, Schopenhauer, Schelling, Goethe, Schiller, Viscer, Carriere and others has descended that school of thought which regards the epic as primarily an expression of the national spirit. . . ."

[25]For a general discussion of the theme of republicanism in the eighteenth century see Gilbert Highet, *The Classical Tradition* (Oxford University Press, 1957), pp. 360-364.

[26]See Ju. F. Florinskaja, "O xudožestvennom metode povesti 'Marfa posadnica'," *XVIII vek,* VIII, pp. 300-301.

[27]Erich Auerbach emphasizes on page 4 of his *Mimesis* (Princeton University Press, 1953) that even though epic characters are individualized personalities, their psyches are described within exhaustively clear and ordered limits.

[28]See C. M. Bowra's discussion of omens in the epic on page 91 of his *Heroic Poetry* (London, 1952).

[29]For detailed discussions of fate in the *Iliad,* see C. M. Bowra's *Tradition and Design in the Iliad* (Oxford, 1930), esp. p. 195 and L. A. Post's, "The Tragic Pattern of the *Iliad," From Homer to Menander* (Berkeley, 1951).

[30]As Georg Lukács says on page 94 of his *The Historical Novel* (London: Merlin Press, 1962), "By concentrating the reflection of life upon a great collision, by grouping all manifestations of life around this collision and permitting them to live themselves out only in relation to the collision, drama simplifies and generalizes the possible attitudes of men to the problems of their lives."

[31]Northrop Frye, *Anatomy of Criticism: Four Essays* (princeton University Press, 1957), 34.

[32]This interpretation of personal issues as useful in reinforcing the work's historical scope varies from the more traditional separation of private and civic themes in the work. Nebel, on page 139 of his *N. M. Karamzin: A Russian Sentimentalist,* refers to private themes as "relegated to the rear." Cross, on page 135 of his *N. M. Karamzin: . . . ,* considers the tale's heroic and personal levels to be unintegrated and even an "essentially unhappy mixture."

[33]Auerbach, *Mimesis,* 6.

[34]See Bowra's discussion of epic description methods on pages 45 and 56 of his *Heroic Poetry.*

[35]*Ibid.,* p. 143.

Index